Sociology in Portugal

DOI: 10.1057/9781137495518.0001

Sociology Transformed

Series Editors: **John Holmwood**, University of Nottingham, UK, and **Stephen Turner**, University of South Florida, US.

'The field of sociology has changed rapidly over the last few decades. *Sociology Transformed* seeks to map these changes on a country by country basis and to contribute to the discussion of the future of the subject. The series is concerned not only with the traditional centres of the discipline, but with its many variant forms across the globe.'

Titles include:

Filipe Carreira da Silva
SOCIOLOGY IN PORTUGAL
A Short History

Anna Larsson and Sanja Magdalenić
SOCIOLOGY IN SWEDEN
A History

Bryan Fanning and Andreas Hess
SOCIOLOGY IN IRELAND
A Brief History

Kirsten Harley and Gary Wickham
AUSTRALIAN SOCIOLOGY
Fragility, Survival, Rivalry

Stephen Turner
AMERICAN SOCIOLOGY
From Pre-Disciplinary to Post-Normal

Sociology Transformed
Series Standing Order ISBN 978-1-137-33817-4 hardback
(*outside North America only*)

You can receive future titles in this series as they are published by placing a standing order. Please contact your bookseller or, in case of difficulty, write to us at the address below with your name and address, the title of the series and the ISBN quoted above.

Customer Services Department, Macmillan Distribution Ltd, Houndmills, Basingstoke, Hampshire RG21 6XS, England

palgrave▸pivot

Sociology in Portugal: A Short History

Filipe Carreira da Silva

Research Fellow, University of Lisbon, Portugal;
Fellow of Selwyn College, Cambridge, UK

palgrave
macmillan

DOI: 10.1057/9781137495518.0001

First published 2016 by
PALGRAVE MACMILLAN

Palgrave Macmillan in the UK is an imprint of Macmillan Publishers Limited, registered in England, company number 785998, of Houndmills, Basingstoke, Hampshire RG21 6XS.

Palgrave Macmillan in the US is a division of St Martin's Press LLC, 175 Fifth Avenue, New York, NY 10010.

Palgrave Macmillan is the global academic imprint of the above companies and has companies and representatives throughout the world.

Palgrave® and Macmillan® are registered trademarks in the United States, the United Kingdom, Europe and other countries.

ISBN: 978-1-137-49552-5 EPUB
ISBN: 978-1-137-49551-8 PDF
ISBN: 978-1-137-49550-1 Hardback

A catalogue record for this book is available from the British Library.

Library of Congress Cataloging-in-Publication Data

Names: Silva, Filipe Carreira da.

Title: Sociology in Portugal: A Short History / Filipe Carreira da Silva.

Description: New York : Palgrave Pivot, 2015. | Includes index.

Identifiers: LCCN 2015037758 | ISBN 9781137495501 (hardback)

Subjects: LCSH: Sociology – Portugal – History – 20th century. | Sociology – Portugal – History – 21st century. | BISAC: SOCIAL SCIENCE / Sociology / General.

Classification: LCC HM477.P67 S55 2015 | DDC 301.09469—dc23

LC record available at http://lccn.loc.gov/2015037758

www.palgrave.com/pivot

DOI: 10.1057/9781137495518

Contents

palgrave▸**pivot**

www.palgrave.com/pivot

Introduction: Sociology in Portugal

Abstract: *This chapter begins with the presentation of the theoretical approach employed to study the history of sociology in Portugal from 1945 to the present day: genealogical pragmatism. This is followed by a discussion of the chief methodological challenges facing such an endeavour. The chapter concludes with a presentation of the five main analytic dimensions of Carreira da Silva's approach: social agents; ideas; instruments; institutions; and contexts.*

Carreira da Silva, Filipe. *Sociology in Portugal: A Short History*. *Basingstoke*: Palgrave Macmillan, 2016. DOI: 10.1057/9781137495518.0002.

At the end of January 1963, the first issue of a new journal in the social sciences called '*Análise Social*' ('Social Analysis') appeared in Lisbon. In retrospect, many will interpret this publication as signalling a crucial first step towards the institutionalization of sociology in Portugal. Nineteen-sixty-three is also the year W.E.B. Du Bois died in Accra, Ghana. Exiled from the United States for his leftist political ideas, at the time of his demise Du Bois was, by and large, ignored by the discipline. Today, however, he is rightly considered one of the founders of American sociology, with works such as *The Philadelphia Negro* (1899), a survey-based depiction of the social conditions of an Afro-American neighborhood, and *The Souls of Black Folk* (1903), perhaps the most accomplished literary achievement ever penned by a sociologist. Back in the US, 1963 is the publication year of Erving Goffman's *Stigma* and Howard Becker's *Outsiders*, but Talcott Parsons' dominance over American sociology was unquestioned. This is not only because of Parsons' work as a social theorist, but also because he was seen 'as an importer' of Weber's ideas about religion and capitalism into the Anglo-Saxon world. Meanwhile, that year in Britain, John H. Goldthorpe and David Lockwood published 'Affluence and the British Class Structure', an article on the consequences of affluence for the working class which would eventually lead to the most celebrated sociological study ever carried out in Britain (Goldthorpe et al., 1968–69). Nineteen-sixty-three is also the heyday of the Frankfurt School of critical theory. This is the year when Adorno published his lecture on 'Culture Industry Reconsidered', Habermas published *Theory and Practice*, and a few months later Marcuse published *One-Dimensional Man*. In Paris, Raymond Aron published his *Eighteen Lectures on Industrial Society*, while Bourdieu began the empirical research on French culture that would eventually lead to his *Distinction* of 1977. This synoptic view of the international context within which sociology in Portugal took its first steps helps us to put this institutional development into perspective. Sociology in the early 1960s was an academic discipline with a long, varied, and discontinuous tradition in a large number of countries, and Portuguese sociologists imported and adapted this well-established and differentiated discipline to local circumstances and problems.

This book is about sociology in Portugal, understood as a national variety of European sociology. The European tradition can be seen as an institutionalized response to the problem of social order in modern capitalist societies in the nineteenth century. Analysed as a 'social contract' between converging individual interests by Enlightenment

DOI: 10.1057/9781137495518.0002

theorists, nineteenth century sociology opted for analysing the forms and structures that are ultimately responsible for making 'society' possible (Eisenstadt 1968). More recently, R.W. Connell suggests a second rationale for the institutionalization of sociology, namely the systematic comparison between Western metropolises and their colonial territories (1997). In the case of sociology in Portugal, the problem which provided the immediate motivation for its institutionalization sprang not so much from the colonial problem, for political reasons which I will detail in the next chapter, but from a 'social question' typical of developing societies – how to use social scientific knowledge for the improvement of social conditions in Western Europe's poorest country.

From this diversity of founding problems, a number of developmental stages may be discerned. In the case of the global development of sociology as an academic discipline, the following can be identified (on periodization see, for instance, Clark 1972): a pre-academic stage, inaugurated by August Comte's coinage of the term 'sociology' and during which organicist and evolutionist models of society proliferated (1830s–90s); the early academic stage, during which sociology first became institutionalized as an academic discipline in universities in Western Europe and the United States (1890s–1900s); the interwar years, marked by the decline of sociology in Europe and the development of the Chicago School (1920s–39s); the post-war renaissance stage, characterized by the revival and definite consolidation of sociology as an academic discipline in Europe and the United States (1945–68), and the current postmodern global stage, marked by the overcoming of modernist paradigms, by increasing internal differentiation, and an unprecedented global scope (1970s–2010s).

The institutional establishment and consolidation of sociology in Portugal I revisit in this book is closely related to these last two stages. This is for two main reasons. First, there is the collaboration between local sociologists and their international peers in terms of training, funding, conferences, research, and publications. Second, theoretical-methodological developments in the discipline abroad provided the framework within which sociology in Portugal was developed. For instance, as in most other small countries, there is no strand of 'Portuguese social theory', if by that one means a cluster of sociologists integrated by common syllabi, a journal, and a research programme as a means to institutionalize intellectual innovation. Sociological theory in Portugal, as I will show below, has been, by and large, an importation of

DOI: 10.1057/9781137495518.0002

ideas from abroad, which were more or less systematically applied to the study of Portuguese society. Individual exceptions, which confirm this diagnosis, include figures such as the Oxford-based Hermínio Martins and critical theorist Boaventura de Sousa Santos.[1]

This last observation invokes an important terminological distinction I make in this book. I distinguish between 'sociology *in* Portugal', in the sense of an academic discipline actually practised in Portugal (sometimes by theorists and educators who are not Portuguese) and which is not focused on the study of Portuguese society, and 'sociology *of* Portugal', in the sense of an epistemic community which defines itself by the sociological, sometimes comparative, study of Portuguese society. In this second sense, one could perhaps speak of a 'Portuguese sociology' as a methodological project whose boundaries are defined by the nation-state called 'Portugal'.[2] For reasons I will make clear below, however, I am of the view that such a designation should be reserved for a handful of national sociologies that, for diverse historical and cultural reasons, developed distinctive ways of doing sociology – a case in point is 'German sociology'. In most other cases, Portugal included, it is more rigorous to speak of sociology *in* that country.

This brings me to the theoretical approach I employ to study sociology in Portugal from 1945 onwards, which is the focus of this book series. Donald N. Levine (1996) has suggested a typology of competing approaches (or narratives) about how sociologists have revisited the discipline's past. These include: a *positivist* approach, whose chief protagonist is Comte and in which social knowledge progresses as metaphysical speculation gradually but inexorably subsides; a *pluralist* narrative first developed in the interbellum period which emphasizes the agonistic plurality of competing viewpoints; a *synthetic* approach in light of which the 'classical' sociological tradition that took shape in turn-of-the-century Western Europe in the writings of seminal figures such as Max Weber and Emile Durkheim converges on a few fundamental sociological principles; a *humanist* genre, quite popular in the 1960s and 1970s, which suggested the existence of yet another 'classical' tradition, this time dating back to the late eighteenth century, constituted by thinkers who first attempted to examine the consequences of the demise of the *ancien régime* and concomitant emergence of modern societies, and a *contextualist* approach, which moves away from the autonomy of the text or ideas to emphasize rather the relevance of social, cultural, ideological, and institutional factors in shaping the meaning of these ideas and texts.

DOI: 10.1057/9781137495518.0002

My approach is contextualist in that I conceive of academic disciplines as being partly shaped by external factors, but it is also genealogical and pragmatic. It is genealogical in the sense that, following Nietzsche and the late Foucault (1971, 1982), I see disciplines as institutionalized struggles over meaning. It is pragmatic in that I do not restrict such struggles over meaning to the level of discourse. Rather, I argue that one needs to take the materiality of the processes of meaning-production seriously. Unlike other pragmatic approaches (e.g. Latour 2005), I do not adopt an anti-humanist stance which sees agency as equally distributed among human and non-human entities. Social agents remain at the heart of my approach, understood as socially embedded organisms oriented to solving concrete action problems within certain external frames, such as academic disciplines themselves, for example. Institutions, academic disciplines included, are not purely social constructs, even though they are socially constructed. They possess a distinctive material form. The dialectic between human agency and this material form can be designated as materiality. In this sense, materiality is the pragmatic response to the pitfalls of both materialism and idealism.

For the purposes of this book, there are two important methodological dualisms I wish to supersede. The first is the one that separates 'discipline history' from 'intellectual history' (Collini 1988), that is to say, this dualism distinguishes 'disciplinary history' from the 'history of disciplines' (Novick 1988). The historian of anthropology George Stocking referred to this dualism when he identified the gulf separating 'internal' histories of disciplines that practitioners told themselves, and 'external' histories by those who mined the disciplines for historical insights (Stocking 1965). Literature on the history of sociology in Portugal has been, by and large, dominated by 'internal' historical studies (Cruz 1983; Nunes 1988; Machado 2009), including case studies of sociology journals (Casanova 1996), sociology conferences (Lobo 1996), or sociology departments (Dias 2006). Several developments in recent decades have contributed to make this dichotomy less salient (Geary 2008). On the one hand, 'internal' accounts have benefited enormously from an ever more sophisticated literature on the history of disciplines. As a result, many practitioners' histories now treat concepts such as tradition, conceptual change, and the construction of disciplinary boundaries in a much more reflexive way. Examples include volumes on history (Novick 1988), sociology (Calhoun 2007), economics (Mirowski 2002), and political science (Adcock, Bevir, and Stimson 2007). Sociologists in Portugal have accompanied this methodological development. 'External' histories by practitioners have emphasized the importance of the Catholic Church in the early period of academic formation (Ferreira 2006), critically discussed its late institutionalization (Hespanha 1996), as well as recent tendencies of internationalization (Fortuna 2008). All these studies share a self-conscious attempt to tread the line between discipline history and intellectual history, and their authors have allegiances both to history and to the discipline they seek to investigate.

On the other hand, an increasing number of studies on the nature of discipline formation, the exercise of specialist expertise, and pedagogy have clarified the dynamics behind the creation and reproduction of academic disciplines. Precursors such as Thomas Kuhn (1962), who shed light on the grounds of scientific communal norms, Michael Polanyi (1958), with his work on the 'tacit knowledge' required for expert practices, as well as more recent contributors such as Warwick (2003), who have helped clarify the 'power of pedagogy' in the creation of scientific communities, have all been central to these developments.

As a result of these changes, an increasing number of scholars work on both sides of the, formerly sharp, divide between internal and external histories of disciplines, and between history and sociology. Illustrating this trend is Andrew Abbott, who has both authored a local history of the Chicago School of sociology (Abbott 1999) and a formal sociology of disciplines (Abbott 2001). Abbott's sociology of disciplines, however, can be criticized on at least two accounts. First, the fractal models Abbott has imported from mathematics are too rigid to capture the actual distribution of power positions in sociology, however elegant they seem. Rather than recurrent nested dichotomies (agency vs. structure, qualitative vs. quantitative, etc.) that structure natural and social sciences alike, I hypothesize the existence, at least in the case of the latter, of distinctively dialogical, uneven, and culturally relative paths of disciplinary development. Second, rather than endless generational recycling of old ideas (Abbott 2001: 17), with little or no space for genuine conceptual innovation, a fuller appreciation of the national dynamics of discipline formation and development would enable Abbott's sociology of disciplines to account for historical discontinuities, Foucault's 'cyclopean moments' ([1971] 1991: 77), such as the one spearheaded by social and political revolution in mid-1970s Portugal.

This last observation brings me to the second methodological dualism I wish to overcome. I refer to the kind of periodization – continuist or

DOI: 10.1057/9781137495518.0002

discontinuist – favoured in one's account. The first wave of studies in the history of sociology in Portugal, written as first-hand testimonies of their authors' roles in the creation and consolidation of sociology, emphasized discontinuity. The change of political regime in the mid-1970s is presented as the pivotal historical break which made academic sociology possible in Portugal (e.g. Nunes 1988, Almeida 1991; Fernandes 1996; Pais and Cabral 2006). A more recent wave of studies, however, suggests a broadly continuist narrative (e.g. Pinto 2004; Neto 2013; Garcia et al. 2015). The most systematic study of sociology in Portugal of the continuist ilk is by Frederico Ágoas (2013), who provides an exhaustive Foucauldian genealogy of the origins of Portuguese sociology since the early twentieth century as a disciplinary form of state power. The historical account I present in this book, however, is explicitly discontinuist in that it emphasizes the fundamental difference between pre-1974 and post-1974 sociology in Portugal. The main reason I do so is empirical. None of the continuist studies indicated above has been able to conclusively demonstrate the influence of early intellectual sources on more recent institutional developments. Determined to find an illustrious early Portuguese sociology, sometimes as early as the 1880s (Machado 1962: 2), these studies incur two of the fallacies that Quentin Skinner has long identified as the pitfalls of the history of ideas, that is, the fallacy of 'anticipation' and the fallacy of 'influence' (1969). Rather than showing a direct causal relationship between the scattered intellectual interventions of the turn of the century and the processes of academic institutionalization of sociology in the late 1960s and early 1970s, they have limited themselves to juxtaposing, as opposed to providing textual evidence that connects, the two. As a result, one of the basic claims I make in this study is that the trajectory of sociology in Portugal is characterized by a fundamental historical discontinuity whose primary cause was a change in the nature of the political regime, that is, the transition to democratic rule than took place in 1974–75 as a result of a leftist military coup.

As noted above, the object of study of this book is an academic discipline. In my view, disciplines are neither the product of the automatic progress of science nor are they 'natural' categories. Rather, disciplines are better understood as projects, in the sense of socially constituted authoritative purveyors of explanations and descriptions of segments of reality. Such projects, as we have seen, are fraught with uncertainties and conflicts. They are also, as Foucault rightly emphasizes (1975), disciplining forces that establish authorities, namely, the state, impose on individuals,

DOI: 10.1057/9781137495518.0002

producing 'docile bodies' and minds. As such, sociology as an academic discipline does not remain external to the subject. Rather, the process of disciplining leads to the internalization of certain values and principles by all those exposed to it, from practitioners to students and the general public. Political theorist Bernard Yack has distinguished between two different senses of the term 'project' (1997: 116–17). On the one hand, a discipline is a project in the sense of a shared aspiration, a collective idea or blueprint. As we shall see in the next chapter, sociology in Portugal in the 1960s was certainly a project in this sense as it denoted a shared generational commitment towards the betterment of social conditions through social scientific means. On the other hand, Yack points to a second meaning of the term. According to the second meaning, disciplines are also projects in the sense of frameworks which provide the boundaries within which agents operate. This second sense of disciplines as systems of constraints is, of course, close to Foucault's understanding of disciplinary power. Historians of the social sciences have explored this second sense of 'disciplinary project' to emphasize the importance of language as the medium through which meaning is produced, namely those systematically integrated bodies of knowledge Foucault designates as 'discursive formations'. It is my contention that sociology in Portugal, much like other social sciences elsewhere, has become a 'discipline' in this double sense. It has always been, with important variations, both a specialized branch of knowledge and an institutionalized form of regulatory control. One of the research questions I pursue in this book is: What sort of project was the project of disciplinary formation in the case of sociology in Portugal?

In order to answer this question, I employ the pragmatic approach described above, taking into account five analytic dimensions. Following Fleck and Dayé (2015), these dimensions are: social agents, ideas, instruments, institutions, and contexts. Let me now briefly introduce each of these dimensions. Agents are often studied individually, that is, intellectual biographies of leading scholars are widely available, as well as autobiographical accounts (e.g. Elias 1994). Another popular unit of analysis are clusters (Clark and Clark 1971), research groups, schools, departments, and universities (Bulmer 1984; Dahrendorf 1995). An even more general unit are generations (Fleck 2011). In this book, I make use of all these units of analysis to account for human agency in the creation and development of sociology in Portugal. Sometimes I discuss individual scholars (such as Sedas Nunes in the next chapter),

DOI: 10.1057/9781137495518.0002

while on other occasions my focus will be upon collectives (as in professional association meetings in the third and fourth chapters), and on other occasions still I will weave individual accounts together to bring about a collective understanding of the discipline as a whole (as in the final chapter). Orienting my analysis on these different occasions are the concrete action problems these social agents (individual or collective) are oriented to, for instance, the problem of internationalization that commands attention in the contemporary period. Responding to a problematic often requires collaboration between a relatively large number of practitioners, which in academic hierarchical contexts such as Continental European instances are typically undertaken under the intellectual orientation and academic patronage of a leader. This is (also) why the analytic distinction individual vs. group can somewhat be obfuscating in the study of academic disciplines.

Ideas will be approached as more or less systematic reflections upon the social world, with a materiality of their own, and articulated with an intent that can at times be political. This understanding of ideas can be contrasted with more traditional approaches that tend to analyse them as free-standing unit-ideas (Nisbet 1970) or theories (Coser 1971), and is closer to Lakatos' concept of a research programme (Lakatos 1970) as in a set of propositions (or ideas) around which agents position themselves, often in conflicting ways. I will show that sociology in Portugal has developed around such struggles over the meaning of certain key sets of ideas or research programmes. As such, ideas can be said to possess an unmistakably performative character. It has been through the learning, teaching, application, discussion, and refinement of ideas that sociologists in Portugal have undertaken their social inquiries, taught their students, while acquiring in the process a distinctive disciplinary identity. From this perspective, sociological ideas are to be studied as much as abstract statements with a certain degree of abstraction and generality as tools of inquiry with a specific embodied materiality. In a crucial sense, then, ideas *make* sociologists. Sociology in Portugal is thus a discursive formation, as Foucault rightly emphasized, but is also much more. It is an institutionalized practice, with a specific materiality, from its outputs in the form of specialized publications to peoples' mores and dress codes.

Instruments, which include specialized libraries, questionnaires, coding handbooks, tape recorders, and cameras, as well as less material instruments such as search strategies, methodologies, and techniques are

DOI: 10.1057/9781137495518.0002

yet another analytic dimension of the present study. At first sight, this may seem surprising. Indeed, it is far more common to analyse instruments when one is talking about the natural sciences, that is, telescopes, microscopes, and so on. Yet as works such as Shapin and Schaffer's *Leviathan and the Air-Pump* (1985) have demonstrated, the divide separating the natural sciences from the human and social sciences is much more porous than we are often led to believe. In actual fact, to endorse a certain method of knowledge production (in their study, Hobbes' naturalist philosophy or Boyle's experimental method) is also to accept a social philosophy. In the case of sociology in Portugal, the choice of instruments reveals not only a certain theoretical and epistemological orientation, but also constitutes a sound indicator of the stage of disciplinary development, that is, the distance separating Sedas Nunes' time-consuming manipulation of his mechanical calculator in the late 1960s (Nunes 1988: 28) and the massification of personal computers and statistical software from the 1990s onwards in Portugal marks not only two distinct historical periods, but also signals the consolidation of a more general orientation towards quantitative methodologies and empiricist epistemologies in both teaching and research in Portugal (on the American case, see Platt 1996).

In this book institutions will be studied from a three-fold perspective which emphasizes their simultaneously constraining and enabling (therefore, *constitutive*) impact upon human agency. First, there are the outlets or physical locations where academic work is conducted, ranging from university departments to academic and professional scientific journals. Second, there are the addressees of the sociological knowledge produced, which can be either other academics or the general public, including state officials, the media, or private contractors. Third, there are the modes of governance which regulate academic politics, which include administrative policies and cultures such as the new public management's audit culture (Strathern 2000). As in most other cases, in the case of sociology in Portugal the state has proved to be a crucial institution, not only by imposing certain modes of governance able to define professional career structures but also by determining groups of public addressees able to dictate research agendas through governmental funding bodies, and providing for the physical installations of sociology departments, research centres, and conference venues (Wagner 1990). A less studied kind of institution is private foundations (Picó 2003: 81–103; Fisher 1993). In the case of Portugal,

DOI: 10.1057/9781137495518.0002

the philanthropic Calouste Gulbenkian Foundation will be shown to have partially complemented the scarcity of public resources available for work in the human and social sciences since the late 1960s, thus providing, at least to a certain extent, an alternative mode of governance to that promoted by the state.

Contexts, the trademark of externalist studies of science, are the final analytic dimension of my study. In particular, I focus upon two types of context that I deem particularly relevant for my purposes. First, I analyse the context of growing internationalization of the social sciences, including sociology, in recent decades. The blueprint for most studies of the internationalization of the science system is still provided by modernization theories of the 1950s, according to which conceptual innovation tends to follow a pattern of diffusion and isomorphism from a given centre to the periphery: hence the analyses of the theoretical-methodological 'Americanization' of the social sciences (Heilbron et al. 2008). As I and a colleague have argued elsewhere, however, I am of the view that a 'varieties of modernity' approach that takes its inspiration from S.N. Eisenstadt's multiple modernities paradigm, provides a more robust explanatory instrument (Silva and Vieira 2009). As I will try to demonstrate, whilst there are certainly tendencies towards 'Americanization' in the shaping of sociology in this case, these were always confronted with competing modernizing sources, namely Western European. For a number of different reasons, Marxism and French sociology were always more important sources of modernization in Portugal than American sociology. As a result, rather than a conception of modernity as ideas and institutional forms emanating from a single centre, it seems to be more realistic to assume the existence of a *variety of modernities*, whose impact often gets entangled once they reach developing countries. This seems to be the case in our interdisciplinary age. From research projects that bring together numerous practitioners in different fields to work side-by-side to resolve a given problem, to large international networks of scientists collaborating in postgraduate programmes and research and development initiatives, the scientific landscape today is no longer dominated by academic disciplines (Abbott 2001). In my view, however, one should be careful when dismissing too readily the organizational function performed by disciplines. Ours may no longer be a 'disciplinary age' per se, but the emerging 'post-disciplinary' era certainly does not preclude a central role for this specific institutional form. As I will try to make clear in this book, disciplines still constitute the backbone of scientific practice, and there is no reason to believe they will cease to do so in the future.

DOI: 10.1057/9781137495518.0002

This brings me to the second context I will take into account in this study, that is, the nation-state. If in the scientific domain academic disciplines are the modern institutional form, very much the same can be said of the territorial nation-state for the political realm. It should thus not come as a surprise that, while in debates on science we are told that we are now living in a post-disciplinary era, an increasing number of political theorists claim that the nation-state is an institutional form of a bygone era. In this case too, I am sceptical of the tendency to dismiss the centrality of the nation-state as a political institution. Even whilst nowadays member-states in the European Union compete with the European Commission for a leading role in the definition and funding of the research agenda, the fact remains that the Portuguese state has consistently performed a central role in the institutionalization of sociology since its very first stages until today. In particular, the change in the character of the political regime will be shown to have impacted in very profound terms the trajectory of this academic discipline in Portugal. The revolutionary transition from a corporatist right-wing dictatorship to a constitutional democratic regime in the mid-1970s marks a fundamental shift in the history of sociology in Portugal. This analysis of corporatism and of a revolutionary democratic transition complements existing analyses of the impact of the Nazi regime (Coser 1984; Ash and Söllner 1996), communist regimes (Keen and Mucha 1994, 2006), and the Cold War on the development of the social sciences (Abbott and Sparrow 2007; Cohen-Cole 2009; Isaac 2007, 2012; Rohde 2013).

Besides secondary data on the Portuguese professional sociological association's membership figures and congresses and other institutional indicators, among the materials employed to support my argument in this book are excerpts from interviews with many of the agents involved in the creation and institutionalization of the discipline in Portugal. This constitutes a rare opportunity to include first-person testimonies, which is only possible owing to the relatively recent academic establishment of sociology in Portugal. Most of these interviewees came of age in the late 1960s and early 1970s.

The book is structured as follows. In the first chapter 'The Early Years, 1945–74', I analyse the conditions of possibility behind the institutionalization of sociology in Portugal, focusing upon how the Grupo de Investigações Sociais (GIS) and its leader, A. Sedas Nunes, responded to the problem of how to create an academic discipline such as sociology under adverse political and economic conditions. This is a period

DOI: 10.1057/9781137495518.0002

characterized by political repression and censorship, colonial war, mass emigration, and profound social and economic issues. These are also the socio-economic and political lenses through which the impact of the Cold War and 'Americanization' was filtered. The following chapter, 'Sociology Institutionalized, 1975–82', revolves around the political regime change of 1974–75 and its consequences for sociology in Portugal. An epoch of leftist revolutionary fervour, this is also when the institutionalization of the academic discipline began, with the first sociology undergraduate degrees and university departments officially recognized by the state authorities. The third chapter, 'Consolidation, 1980s–1990s', discusses an intermediary phase of institutional development framed by European integration, democratic consolidation, and economic turmoil. This is when the first professional association was created alongside the proliferation of postgraduate programmes, sociology departments, and journals. The fourth chapter, 'Internationalization, 1995 to the Present Day', focuses upon the current phase of institutional development. Internationalization is the main problematic of this stage, constituting a challenge to individual and collective ways of teaching, applying for research funding, and publishing findings. The fifth chapter, 'Sociology's Voices', presents excerpts from 16 interviews with Portuguese sociologists who address the successive phases, circumstances, agents, and institutions involved in the development of sociology as an academic discipline. The imaginary conversation that emerges is a fascinating collective discourse addressing the different developmental stages, conflicting theoretical orientations, and multiple thematic specializations that compose contemporary Portuguese sociology. I conclude with some brief remarks on the current situation of austerity after the financial crisis and its implications for universities and sociology in particular.

Notes

1   But see, for instance, Guibentif (2010) and Fernandes (1993, 2008).
2   The notion of 'methodological nationalism' was first articulated, of course, by Hermínio Martins (1974: 276f.). On recent re-examinations of this concept, see Wimmer and Schiller (2002), Chernilo (2006). See also Beck (2000).

DOI: 10.1057/9781137495518.0002

1
The Early Years, 1945–74

Abstract: *This chapter covers the post-war period when, whilst still not formally recognized as an academic discipline, sociology began to enjoy independent scholarly production in Portugal. The right-wing dictatorship of Salazar and Caetano is analysed as the impeding factor. The strategies of social agents, namely the case of Adérito Sedas Nunes and the cluster of students around him, will illustrate my argument. Institutions, including the state, private foundations, and academic journals, will also be considered.*

Carreira da Silva, Filipe. *Sociology in Portugal: A Short History*. Basingstoke: Palgrave Macmillan, 2016. DOI: 10.1057/9781137495518.0003.

DOI: 10.1057/9781137495518.0003

Lisbon, January 1963. The first issue of a new social sciences journal is published, inaugurating an institutional trajectory that would lead, in little over a decade, to the creation of the first departments and under-graduate sociology degrees in Portugal. The new journal was entitled *Análise Social* ('Social Analysis'), its title echoing an existing journal of economics entitled *Análise Económica* ('*Economic Analysis*').[1] This journal provided a crucial institutional outlet around which A. Sedas Nunes was able to mobilize the intellectual efforts of a group of young scholars, mostly economists, all of them Catholic, to respond to the problem of the day, that is, to expose through social-scientific means the abhorrent social problems confronting one of the last fascist regimes in the world.

Portugal was, at the time, one of the most rural societies in Western Europe and also the poorest. Between 1954 and 1960, the annual growth rate (constant prices) of GDP was 4.3%, reaching 6.9% between 1960 and 1973 (Rocha 1984: 621). These robust economic growth rates, however, were partly a statistical illusion. The fact was that Salazar's 'Estado Novo' calamitously failed to realize social justice. Until 1974, the state had been both unwilling and unable to take responsibility for redistribution and social welfare provision. Welfare services chronically lacked financial, human, and technical resources to implement even residual policies, and were expected to back up the status quo. Yet with very limited access to socio-economic indicators and very few publication outlets available to make these findings known, the gargantuan task facing the socially progressive group of social scientists around Sedas Nunes was to *show* this was indeed the case. It was, therefore, a matter of exposing social realities hitherto hidden from the population itself. Of course, to make social issues known was a delicate political matter in a repressive politi-cal regime such as Salazar's. This was, in brief, the fine line the founders of sociology in Portugal had to negotiate in the 1960s. On the one hand, to create the institutional conditions so that sociological instruments could be employed to expose social problems typical of developing societies such as poverty, emigration, unemployment, labour conflicts, lack of sanitation, and so on. And on the other hand, to be politically astute enough to evade the censorship apparatus of the regime, which often meant exercising self-censorship in the dissemination of findings. This political gamble posed a wrenching moral dilemma, as later auto-biographical statements make clear. To choose to remain in the country and pursue an academic career within the strict confines defined by the authorities, especially in face of a growing number of political exiles and

DOI: 10.1057/9781137495518.0003

political prisoners, risked being regarded in some quarters as 'collabora-tionism'. Yet without it, the chances of the regime allowing sociology to be institutionalized, which Salazar himself considered to be 'socialism under disguise' (Nunes 1988: 37), were simply non-existent.

The situation in other Western countries at the time could have hardly been more different, which contributed to the perception many Portuguese shared that they were living in an 'anomalous' regime with no less 'anomalous' modes of governance of scientific activity. The 1960s marked the zenith of self-confidence and intellectual authority of the social sciences in the US and Western Europe. This modernist vision of the role of the social sciences fed upon: 'the defeat of fascism, the disintegration of colonial empires, and the threat of communism' (Ross 2015: 229). By contrast, in the 1960s Portugal fascism was yet to be defeated, the colonial empire still stretched from the Atlantic shores of Africa to Southeast Asia, and the threat of communism only rein-forced the regime's rhetoric of self-preservation. The US, benefiting from having emerged from World War II as the strongest world power and having evaded both fascism and communism, was busy promoting its products, science and technology among them. Important institu-tional outlets that sustained the projection of America's cultural values and institutional forms included private foundations, disciplinary organizations, universities, and government agencies. In particular, the American model of the research university, under which teaching and research are pursued within the same institution, provided a powerful pole of attraction for modernizing countries. Likewise, the disciplinary form of American social science was being actively promoted by inter-national organizations such as UNESCO. The 'Americanization' of the social sciences in Western Europe varied widely, of course. Swedish Social Democrats, for instance, emulated American paradigms as they found Parsons' structural-functionalism compatible with their own vision of an integrated, harmonious egalitarian society. By contrast, with a university mode of governance with little or no disciplinary autonomy, Italy offered a far less welcoming context for the American model. Likewise, in Portugal, despite the best efforts of government agencies such as the CIA to provide discreet support to the nascent social sciences (Nunes 1988: 41), 'Americanization' has always been limited at best. As a result, sociology in Portugal first developed around a materialist problematic of structural constraints on practical action, leading sociologists to study such topics as structure, class relations,

DOI: 10.1057/9781137495518.0003

change, or power, but to downplay quintessential American concerns such as deviance and values.

A second important context to take into account when considering the formation of sociology as an academic discipline is the system of academic disciplines, i.e. how sociology fared vis-à-vis other human and social sciences in its dealings with the state. As in other colonial empires, anthropology and history in Portugal had long and distinguished academic records (Pinto 2004: 14–15). Alongside management and administration and tropical medicine, these human and social-scientific discourses provided precious knowledge of colonial territories, their populations and cultures under Portuguese rule. By contrast, critical knowledge of the social conditions of the metropolitan society was anything but helpful. Yet sociology needs not be critical. In France, the conservative sociological school founded by Frédéric Le Play had long competed for disciplinary dominance with the Durkheimian school (Bannister 2005: 346). Given that since the nineteenth century France acted like a cultural magnet for successive generations of Portuguese intellectual elites, it should come as no surprise that one of the very few sociological initiatives allowed under the fascist regime was a short-lived LePlaysian experiment whose protagonist was the Belgian Paul Descamps (see Cruz 1983; Ágoas 2013: 225–27; Neto 2013: 46). Despite the ideological proximity between Descamps' LePlaysian sociology and Salazar's corporative principles and social Catholic ideas, however, the application of this sociological approach to legitimize the regime's own policies was not successful (Hespanha 1996: 5), and left virtually no trace in subsequent attempts to introduce sociology into the Portuguese academic curriculum.

This LePlaysian experiment, of course, may have been influenced by Sedas Nunes' Catholic background and his own writings on the Social Doctrine of the Church (Nunes 1961). In fact, however, Sedas Nunes always maintained a careful distance between his writings and ideas on theological doctrine and his work as a social scientist. As a consequence, there is virtually no reference in Sedas Nunes' sociological works to any of the LePlaysian antecedents that today's internalist historians of sociology in Portugal are so keen to document. In general, in what constitutes a notable distinction from the Irish case, there was never a Catholic sociology in Portugal as such, in the sense of a long-standing, influential, and institutionally visible tradition of sociological thinking and research. The partial exception are the studies of Portuguese churchgoers promoted by

DOI: 10.1057/9781137495518.0003

the Catholic Church since the 1950s (Ferreira 2006; see also Silva 1996), but again these had virtually no impact upon the studies conducted by Sedas Nunes and the GIS in the 1960s and early 1970s and are, therefore, only of antiquarian interest.

The main problem driving this Portuguese cluster of early sociological precursors was that of development, namely of fostering development in a backward society through social scientific means. This motivation was at once moral-political and social-scientific. It had originally emerged in the 1950s out of a social progressive Catholic milieu genuinely concerned with the betterment of social conditions among the most vulnerable segments of society, and gradually became a social-scientific quest that would: 'contribute to change and the betterment of conditions in society' (Nunes 1988: 50–51). If there was a unifying interest mobilizing this group of young scholars it was that of studying social problems, in the general sense of problems of development. If there was an intellectual inclination, it was that of sheer intellectual curiosity about social realities (Nunes 1988: 19).

This is well illustrated by Sedas Nunes' first 'sociological adventure' (1988: 28) on the dualist nature of Portuguese society (Nunes 1964; see also 2000). First published in a special issue of *Análise Social* on the 'social aspects of economic development in Portugal', this article mobilized an unprecedented range of statistical figures to characterize and interpret the process of socio-economic change in post-war Portugal. The essay's main thesis may now seem trivial – that Portugal was better understood as a two-speed society, as it were, with a 'traditional' backward countryside and geographically circumscribed 'modern' poles around Lisbon and Oporto (1964: 420). However, in 1960s Portugal it was pathbreaking. The mobilization of statistical figures to quantify social conditions was something virtually unheard of, let alone their usage to explain sociologically Portugal's development problems and to suggest concrete solutions to pressing social issues such as the so-called 'rural exodus' from the 'traditional' countryside to the 'modern' capital (1964: 456). Indeed, the essay 'Portugal, sociedade dualista' proved pivotal in turning Sedas Nunes into a sociological authority almost overnight (1988: 39).

It would be a serious mistake, however, to depict the early sociological endeavours of Sedas Nunes (e.g. 1965) and his cluster as a well-intentioned, straightforward success. To begin with, today's reader may react with incredulity to their focus upon the developmental problems of a country located in Western Europe, while that same country at the time headed a colonial empire composed of large territories with far more acute social problems. Did Connell not show that sociology was born in Western Europe out of a systematic comparison with its colonial possessions? At best, this may account for certain cases such as that of French sociology, but it certainly fails to capture the realities of non-democratic colonial powers such as Portugal. In fact, this sort of intra-imperial sociological inquiry was simply off-limits. Both the colonial empire and the nature of the political regime, as Sedas Nunes was keenly aware, were taboos whose violation meant political sanctioning eventually leading to institutional boycott, forced exile, or prison sentences (Nunes 1988: 25). This is how Sedas Nunes described the self-censorship he had been forced to impose upon himself and those around him in the late 1960s so that the first sociological works would pass the regime's official censorship:

> Some of the young scholars that came to work at GIS assumed that we, especially me, only said and published in the journal what we did because that was all we had to say and wanted to publish. They were not aware of the limitations imposed upon us from the exterior. As a result, they too wanted to say and publish everything they saw fit. That I could not allow. I had to 'correct' their texts with them as to make them 'publishable'. The nefarious regime that is no more forced my hand. I think that they eventually understood that the intellectual tortures I imposed on them were the same I imposed on myself. But I cannot forget the role I had to perform, neither my face before them. Sometimes I wonder whether it would not have been preferable to tell them simply: 'What you have written cannot be published' and publish nothing of what they had written. But I have always wanted to go to the extreme limit of the tolerable, to explore all dimensions and frontiers of the possible and of the sayable. Maybe it was a mistake … even today I feel the need to excuse myself. (1988: 27)

These words suffice to illustrate the difficult political circumstances of 'conditioned liberty', as Sedas Nunes euphemistically put it elsewhere (2013: 9), in which his GIS developed its first sociological activities. Indeed, the relationship between the Portuguese government and the incipient sociological cluster around Sedas Nunes was far from straightforward and transparent. If, as we have seen, fascist authorities imposed strict limits upon what could be said and published, it is no less true that the transition from Salazar to Marcelo Caetano's rule in 1969 brought with it a certain hope of political openness. Of course, this was no regime change, but only an attempt by certain forces within the regime

DOI: 10.1057/9781137495518.0003

to promote changes in order to keep the regime going in increasingly adverse international conditions. Among these changes was the new role of the social sciences. Taking its inspiration from the technocratic model of the post-war social sciences, disciplines such as sociology were now seen by certain segments of the regime as instruments of enlightened social change. The risk for social scientists, of course, was that of being instrumentalized, i.e. of assisting Caetano to extend his hold on power and thus preventing (or, at least, delaying) the transition to democratic rule. Again, Sedas Nunes was keenly aware of this risk.

This much is clear from his account of the historical origins of the research centre GIS and the journal *Análise Social*. Both institutional outlets were the product, he tells us, of an 'improbable triangle' (1988: 18) composed of one group, one man, and one politician. The 'group' was, of course, those young Catholic economists who revolved about him. Sedas Nunes depicts them as a group that became politically aware of the social issues confronting their society during their undergraduate years, and despite being disillusioned with Salazarism, were seen by the regime as: 'intelligent, competent, and especially with "good manners", i.e. well trained in the religious and moral principles of the Catholic, Apostolic and Roman Holy Mother Church' (Nunes 1988: 17). The 'man' was an academic, José Pires Cardoso, perhaps the most systematic analyst of corporatist doctrine[2] in Portugal and director of the 'Gabinete de Estudos Corporativos' (GEC, Centre for Corporatist Studies). Also disillusioned with the regime, which failed to implement his ideas, Cardoso turned his energies from the mid-1950s to the study of social problems. This established academic figure, with close ties to the upper echelons of the regime, acted as the patron of Sedas Nunes and the GIS, a body which originated as a sub-unit of the GEC. The 'politician' was the Minister of Corporations and Social Welfare, José João Gonçalves de Proença. After consulting with Pires Cardoso, Gonçalves de Proença eventually promulgated the decree creating the 'Gabinete de Investigações Sociais' and, with it, *Análise Social*.

As the intervention by the third element of the 'improbable triangle' makes clear, the risk of being manipulated by the regime was also present regarding funding for the professionalization of Sedas Nunes and the members of his cluster. In short, there were two clusters. The first GIS was created in 1963 and was composed of five members (Sedas Nunes, Raul da Silva Pereira, Mário Murteira, Mário Pinto, and Alfredo de Sousa, all of them economists, with Maria Manuela Silva and Mário

DOI: 10.1057/9781137495518.0003

Cardoso dos Santos joining the initial group later). The second GIS emerged in the late 1960s, adding to the first group a number of scholars trained in law, economics, engineering, agronomy, philosophy, history, colonial administration and so on. This was only possible owing to the financial support gathered by Sedas Nunes from private and state sources. Part of the funding came from the Calouste Gulbenkian Foundation, a charitable organization created in 1956 by a Portugal-based oil magnate of Armenian origin. In 1964 the Foundation awarded Sedas Nunes a research grant, enabling him to pursue an independent research career of sorts, and two years later the Foundation began to fund a number of junior research fellows to join Sedas Nunes. This is how the second GIS came about. Decisive support for the professionalization of this cluster came from the government, specifically following the political death of Salazar in 1968.[3] With Caetano in power, the social and political genera-tion to which Sedas Nunes belonged saw their standing reinforced. As a result, he applied to three governmental agencies for institutional support and swiftly received it. In 1969 GIS signed three protocols with each agency and was granted ten fully funded posts for its research staff. This arrangement remained in place until the democratic revolution of 1974. Fearful of being politically associated with the fascist regime, all the research staff resigned a few months after the revolution (1988: 49). Another source of state funding came from a government social welfare agency, which redirected contributions towards pension reform to fund social-scientific research (1988: 40). In short, as Sedas Nunes summa-rizes: 'GIS always subsisted through state funding, and *Análise Social* was always paid for with state funding' (2013: 16).

Besides the state and a private foundation, there was a third source of funding. This was the Congress for the Freedom of Culture, an anti-communist cultural front established in Berlin in 1950. As a member of the Portuguese committee of the congress, Sedas Nunes benefited from its financial support to fund workshops, the participation of several research fellows in international meetings, as well as a lengthy research stay in Paris. This all came to an end abruptly. In April 1966 a five-article series in the *New York Times* revealed that the CIA was the major source of funding of the Congress (Mudrovcic 1997). With its apolitical façade fatally exposed, the funding activities of the Congress rapidly dwindled. Portugal was no exception. Despite the regime's proximity to the anti-communist agenda of the Congress, Lisbon always sought to occupy a position equidistant between Washington and Moscow. As a result, much

DOI: 10.1057/9781137495518.0003

to Sedas Nunes' dissatisfaction, the Congress' funding of the nascent Portuguese social sciences dried up in the following months (1988: 41). However, the relationships and collaborative links Congress funding had made possible persisted.

This is especially true of Paris, where Sedas Nunes and certain of his students had been able to establish academic relationships. In fact, French sociology was arguably the main source of inspiration as far as sociological theories and methodologies were concerned. Sedas Nunes writes in the late 1980s: 'As to foreign sources, unlike what happens nowadays, in the 1960s academics lived off French culture. It was French ideological, intellectual and political trends that were imported to Portugal' (2013: 22). This was for three reasons. First, there was the long-standing historical tradition of influence I have already alluded to. Second, French social thinking in the 1960s was of exceptional stature, with a concentration of high-calibre figures such as Sartre, Braudel, Foucault, Lacan, Dumont, and in sociology, Gurvitch, Aron, Stoetzel, and Touraine. The decade marked the demise of existentialism and the heyday of the academic prestige of the structuralist movement (Benoist 1978; Kurzweil 1978), with Lévi-Strauss (1963, 1973) as its main figure. Third, there are the numerous personal contacts established with French sociologists, sometimes facilitated by Portuguese graduate students in Paris (see Chapter 5), who agreed to teach one-week open courses, that is, courses designed to be appropriate for all students and the general public.[4] Alain Touraine taught an open course on sociology of development, Serge Hurtig a course on political sociology, Henri Mendras a course on rural sociology and one on the rural exodus, Jean-Daniel Reynaud a course on sociology of work and one on modern industrial society.

Much like the Soviet Union's 'glasnost' 20 years later, the 'glasnost' of the Estado Novo would do little to prevent the fall of the regime.[5] The 1973 oil crisis and the ensuing inflationary pressure on commodity prices dealt a devastating blow to the already fragile economy, exhausted by a 13-year war effort in Africa. Soon afterwards, on 25 April 1974 a military coup brought down the 48-year-old dictatorship of Salazar and Caetano, which had opposed the institutionalization of sociology until the bitter end. This meant that sociological theories and methodologies were first taught under other names. From 1972, ISCTE offered an undergraduate degree in 'labour sciences' which in effect was a degree in sociology but for its name. Its staff was composed of GIS members led by Sedas Nunes, who found in ISCTE an institutional outlet that enabled them to begin teaching sociology to an undergraduate pool of students for the

DOI: 10.1057/9781137495518.0003

first time. A few months after the coup, a university general assembly at ISCTE proposed to reconvert the 'labour sciences' degree into a sociology degree proper. In 1974 the Minister of Education Sottomayor Cardia officially endorsed this decision in the form of a decree.

No less important at this juncture was the return of political exiles. A whole generation had left the country for destinations such as France, Belgium, Switzerland, the UK, and Italy, either to avoid serving in the colonial war or being subject to political repression (Fernandes 1996: 18). The most distinguished Portuguese sociologist in exile was Hermínio Martins. Born in Mozambique in 1934 and exiled in Britain since the 1950s, Martins' work stands out as one of the few internationally recognized sociological analysis of the country (1969, 1971). The reception of his ideas in Portugal, however, has remained limited to this day. In the days and weeks after the coup, Portugal witnessed the return of many of these exiles, among them a few dozen social scientists. Sociology in Portugal began as an institutionally recognized academic discipline as an outcome of the complex political milieu of the late 1960s and early 1970s, and its main agents were Sedas Nunes, the first and second GIS, and the political exiles who joined them. It is in this sense that Sedas Nunes sums up the historical origins of sociology in Portugal. The ISCTE and the Institute of Social Sciences, the successor of the original GIS, were: 'two branches of the same tree, a tree whose seed was buried in the ground when, at the end of January 1963, the first issue of "Análise Social" came out' (1988: 46).

Notes

1   *Análise Económica*, directed by Francisco Pereira de Moura.
2   Sedas Nunes' first book was also on corporatist doctrine. See Nunes (1954).
3   In August 1968 Salazar suffered a concussion as a result from falling from a chair. Salazar's 'fall from the chair' came to represent his political fall. A few months later, Salazar suffered a stroke and eventually died in 1970.
4   These open courses took place in different locations, first, in the ISCEF ('Instituto Superior de Ciências Económicas e Financeiras', today's ISEG), then in the Calouste Gulbenkian Foundation, and later in the Institute of Social Studies that would become the ISCTE in 1972.
5   On the relationship between the political regime and the social sciences, see Graham and Makler (1979).

DOI: 10.1057/9781137495518.0003

2
Sociology Institutionalized, 1975–82

Abstract: *This chapter focuses upon the birth of sociology in Portugal as a fully recognized academic discipline following the left-wing revolutionary democratic transition of 1974–75. The return of a generation of exiled social scientists, including sociologists, from Switzerland, France, and elsewhere is analysed. Within a few years, all four major centres of production of sociological knowledge would be established – ISCTE, New University, CES, and the ICS. Each of these centres would eventually develop a distinct institutional understanding of sociology. A new journal was created – Revista Crítica de Ciências Sociais (1978) – which would play an important role in critical sociology. The chapter concludes with a reference to the institutionalization of sociology in the context of the early 1980s.*

Carreira da Silva, Filipe. *Sociology in Portugal: A Short History*. Basingstoke: Palgrave Macmillan, 2016. DOI: 10.1057/9781137495518.0004.

Here I focus upon the birth of sociology as a fully recognized academic discipline following the left-wing revolutionary democratic transition of 1974–75. Within a few years, all four major centres of production of sociological knowledge would be established – ISCTE, New University, CES, and the ICS. Each of these centres would eventually develop a distinct institutional understanding of sociology. A new journal was created – *Revista Crítica de Ciências Sociais* (1978) – which would play an important role in critical sociology. Particular attention will be given to the return of a generation of exiled social scientists, including sociologists, from Switzerland, France, and elsewhere.

For most of its modern history, Portugal was a country oriented not towards Europe, but towards the Atlantic. An imperial power, Portuguese society had closer cultural ties with geographically distant territories such as Brazil or Goa than with neighbouring Spain, which was more often perceived as a military threat rather than an economic opportunity. All this changed with the democratic transition in 1974–75. For the first time in centuries, Portuguese society turned to Europe rather than the Atlantic as its natural, privileged geopolitical context. As with all collective gestalt switches, this too was not without its contradictions, ambivalences, and blind spots.

This fundamental reorientation in outlook was a consequence of the change in political regime. The change in political regime was, in turn, a crucial element in the institutional trajectory of sociology in Portugal. The fact that this was a revolutionary democratic transition helps one understand the discontinuity in the academic institutionalization of sociology. The contrast with Spain, where the transition to democracy was a negotiated political process that unfolded between Franco's death in 1975 and the Spanish Constitution of 1978, is instructive. In Spain, the Franco regime, despite its strict surveillance of the universities, allowed the development of a functionalist sociology, predominantly empirical in nature. As a result, from the early 1960s, a considerable stock of data and expertise about Spanish social conditions accumulated. In 1963 two institutional landmarks appeared: an official Institute of Public Opinion was set up (which later became the 'Centro de Investigaciones Sociológicas', CIS), and the journal '*Revista Española de Opinión Pública*' (later, '*Revista Española de Investigaciones Sociológicas*', REIS) was published for the first time. This period of functionalist hegemony in Spain saw the expansion of sociology in the universities and the proliferation of private foundations and social research agencies. The negotiated transition to

DOI: 10.1057/9781137495518.0004

democracy of 1975–78 changed very little in the institutionalization of sociology in Spain. The main difference was, of course, the new opportunities afforded to Marxist and critical sociologies from the 1980s onwards (Giner and Yrulea 2015: 381–82). By contrast, there was virtually no sociology degree in Portugal during the Estado Novo, American-style functionalist sociology was virtually unheard of, and the few incipient institutional initiatives discussed in the previous chapter were developed under extremely difficult political, economic, and moral conditions. All this began to change, however, with the new political regime. These changes in the institutionalization of sociology in Portugal are the topic of this chapter.

The main context, as indicated above, is political. Portugal in the mid-1970s went through a social and political revolution dominated by leftist ideologies. There was an upsurge of revolutionary fervour across the country that conflicting political forces, including military forces, attempted to mobilize in their favour. It was also a period characterized by intense political and social mobilization, with particularly expressive imagery associated with it. This was the zenith of popular street art, to which the public imagery of the 2008 Great Recession continually refers back to. In such contexts, institutional procedures tend to be hampered. Repetition, predictability, routines are all put under strain by revolutionary forces, whose legitimation is not instrumental rationality or legality but democratic fervour and popular assent. At the same time, revolutionary fervour allows for rapid institutional change and innovation. This is exactly what happened in Portugal. In a few years a new Constitution had been drafted and approved (Vieira and Silva 2013), competitive general and local elections had taken place, and sweeping administrative reform was under way. Universities were part and parcel of general reform of the institutional apparatus of the Portuguese state. Leftist ideological fervour led to political purges across the administration, including academia. This, in turn, reinforced opportunities for the institutionalization of the social sciences, namely those whose antecedents, or lack of antecedents, offered secure progressive, emancipatory, left-wing credentials such as sociology. In a way, the absence of a functionalist tradition such as that in Spain worked in sociology's favour in Portugal, especially because of the rather odd circumstance, given the right-wing nature of the Estado Novo, that Marxism had been a central reference point since the late 1960s (e.g. Nunes 2013: 22; Pinto 2004: 15). In 1974 sociology had both the right historical antecedents (unlike, for instance, anthropology

DOI: 10.1057/9781137495518.0004

whose colonial ties could be politically sensitive) and a most favourable epistemological orientation.

The revolutionary context in which sociology began to be established in Portugal contrasts heavily with the international scene. The 1970s were characterized by the erosion of the post-war authority that the social sciences had enjoyed. Social and political upheavals in the US and Europe in the 1960s, including the civil rights movement, student riots, and the rise of feminism, positively shattered the post-war consensus around which the social sciences had been established. The main targets of these changes were, of course, the liberal functionalist premises of sociology and political science. In the meantime, the independence of former colonial territories triggered a postcolonial dynamic that fundamentally questioned the legitimacy of the gaze of functionalist anthropology. As for funding, the 1970s were the peak decade of federal government support to science. With it came a shift towards commissioned research, where the research goals are set not by the researcher but by the funding body. The National Science Foundation became the major source of science funding, hence imposing a natural sciences model of research (quantitative methodologies, practical purposes) on the social sciences. The 1970s also witness the rise of postmodernism as an international intellectual movement. The modernist project of the social sciences that reigned through the post-war period (see e.g. Wagner 1994: 104–22) suddenly becomes the target of the discontents of modern society, whose grievances could be traced back to Freud, Marx, and Nietzsche. Parsons' structural-functionalist paradigm, which had virtually no influence upon Portuguese sociologists, soon became the target of this new postmodern generation of sociologists. But so did Marx, especially if interpreted through structuralist lenses. Hence the focus on the early Marx in Anglo-Saxon conflict sociology. But even the Marx of the *Economic and Philosophic Manuscripts of 1848* proved too modern for this new generation, given Marx's notions of essence, species being, and so on. It was Nietzsche who would eventually become the key inspiration for critical sociologists from the 1980s onwards, at least among Western thinkers (see Sousa Santos' interview in Chapter 5), thus facilitating the turn to culture and identity politics that characterize sociology today.

Whilst aware of these international developments, the social agents who played key roles in the institutionalization of sociology in Portugal were confronted with a specifically Portuguese problem. The main dilemma they faced was not that of redefining well-established paradigms

DOI: 10.1057/9781137495518.0004

and entrenched research models as in France or the US, but one of institution building. Similar to what happened in the political domain, with a whole new political-administrative edifice being designed and built to replace what was there before, the change of political regime in 1974–75 offered Portuguese social scientists a once in a lifetime opportunity to create training courses and research centres in sociology almost from scratch.

For those who had been based in Portugal since the 1960s, such as Sedas Nunes and his cluster, this meant continuing to use their knowledge of foreign sources to pursue their academic activities in the open for the first time. But there were also those who were aware of the international scene since they had direct contact with many of these foreign sources and intellectual circles. As we saw in the previous chapter, political repression and the colonial war led thousands to leave the country from the early 1960s onwards. Many returned in the aftermath of the revolution, including dozens of social scientists. With them came the expertise they had accumulated in graduate studies abroad. In particular, this diaspora of political exiles utilized 1970s French social thinking and sociological methodologies, much more than contemporary German, Italian, or Anglo-American traditions, to form the theoretical-methodological blueprint for the first degrees in sociology in Portugal.

The first Portuguese sociology degree dates from 1974 and its home institution was the ISCTE, a higher education institute whose main area of studies is management sciences. As we know, this degree was organized around Sedas Nunes' cluster and developed with the help of numerous exiles including Manuel Villaverde Cabral, João Freire, among others. The basic matrix upon which the degree was organized was that of historical materialism, with a strong emphasis upon class analysis, social change, social structures, and social practices. With a few important exceptions, retaining this broadly materialist orientation, Pierre Bourdieu's genetic structuralism became the paradigm around which most teaching at ISCTE was undertaken from the 1980s. This Bourdieusian orientation continues to be found behind most sociological research developed at the 'Centro de Investigações e Estudos Sociológicos' (CIES), ISCTE's research centre for sociology. A second, arguably less prominent, influence is Anthony Giddens, namely his 1990s collaborative project with Ulrich Beck and Scott Lash on reflexive modernization. Sociology degree at ISCTE remains the largest and most reputed in Portugal to this day.

DOI: 10.1057/9781137495518.0004

In 1979 a second degree in sociology was established at the New University of Lisbon.[1] One of the founding figures was Vitorino Magalhães Godinho. Godinho was perhaps the most important Portuguese historian of the twentieth century whose political views forced him to leave the country between 1962 and 1974. A member of the 'Annales' school (Cardoso 2011), Godinho utilizes structuralism to reconstruct the economic and social history of Portuguese maritime expansion with a clear political intent – that of providing an alternative basis for Portuguese identity that went beyond Salazar's fascist ideology (Tomich 2005). His magisterial structuralist historical works (Godinho 1943–46, 1946, 1955, 1963, 1967, 1990) were written during a three-decade career at French academic institutions. Partly funded by the Ford Foundation, Godinho worked first at the CNRS between 1947 and 1960, then at Clermont-Ferrand University between 1970 and 1974. Upon his return to Portugal, Godinho had a brief stint as Minister of Education and Culture (1974), during which he assisted Sedas Nunes to consolidate the financial stability of the GIS until 1982, but soon returned to academia. In 1975 he helped found the Faculty of Social and Human Sciences, where he directed the Centre for Studies in Sociology (CESNOVA), in which he tried to implement the model of the famous VI Section of the *École Pratique des Hautes Études* (today, *École des Hautes Études en Sciences Sociales*). It is in this institutional and cultural milieu that the second degree in sociology in Portugal was created. Hence the return of political exiles became of great importance. A case in point is that of António Barreto, exiled to Geneva between 1963 and 1974. After a brief political career in the aftermath of the revolution, Barreto was one of the degree's founders, eventually moving to ICS in the early 1980s. Unsurprisingly, the original orientation of this degree was markedly different from that of ISCTE. Rather than materialist class analysis, Weberian historical sociology provided the central theoretical-methodological orientation of Nova's sociology degree. This relative openness towards the comparative study of culture, values, and institutions, as illustrated by its reception of Eisenstadt's work (e.g. 2007), is one of the distinctive features of the Faculty of Social and Human Sciences and of CESNOVA to this day.

Boaventura de Sousa Santos is the third founding figure of sociology in Portugal. Originally trained in law and coming from a socially progressive Catholic background similar to that of Sedas Nunes and his cluster, Santos began his academic career as a university lecturer at the Law Faculty of the University of Coimbra in the mid-1960s. Like

DOI: 10.1057/9781137495518.0004

many of his generation, Santos benefitted from a scholarship from the Gulbenkian Foundation to pursue his studies abroad. His political and scientific orientation underwent a decisive turn during his graduate studies in the US. Santos obtained a PhD in sociology of law from Yale in 1973, with both a strong ethnographic component (gleaned from experience of a favela in Rio de Janeiro) and a prominent critical orientation. These features characterized his sociological programme from that point onwards. In 1973 he helped found the Economics Faculty of the University of Coimbra, where in 1988 a sociology degree would be created. But a research component has always been the pivotal element around which the Coimbra school of critical sociology revolves (e.g. Santos 1977). In 1978 two important institutional outlets were created – the Centre for Social Studies (Centro de Estudos Sociais, CES) and the journal *Revista Crítica de Ciências Sociais* (RCCS) – both directed by Santos from the beginning. These two outlets provided Santos and his cluster with the institutional means through which to build a critical alternative to the materialist and historical-comparative sociologies based in Lisbon. More important, if these two are unmistakably modernist in their epistemological orientation, the Coimbra school was one of the early strongholds of postmodernist social sciences in Portugal (Santos 1987, 1989). Another distinctive trait of Santos' work is that he is one of the few Portuguese sociologists to have developed an original theoretical approach (e.g. Santos 1994, 2000). This enabled Santos and his cluster to eventually move in the 1980s beyond postmodernist concerns around the nature of knowledge to an original postcolonial, critical social theory. This original strand of critical theory, first articulated in the 1990s and still in the making today, draws heavily upon empirical and theoretical contributions from the Global South. An important institutional outlet to support this agenda is the CES-Almedina book series, which has complemented the journal RCCS as a means to disseminate this research. The main topics, typically articulated in interdisciplinary terms, include cities and architecture, knowledge and institutions, democracy and participation, law and society, identities and intercultural dialogues, literature and the arts, social policies, risk and regulation, and work and society.

A fourth founding figure of sociology in Portugal is based in Oporto – José Madureira Pinto. Having joined GIS in 1971, Pinto followed Sedas Nunes into ISCTE and ISCEF as a lecturer. Soon, however, he relocated to Oporto, never to return to Lisbon. In 1974 Pinto began teaching at the Economics Faculty of the University of Oporto where he helped create

DOI: 10.1057/9781137495518.0004

a research centre in sociology. Ten years later, in 1984, Pinto founded '*Cadernos de Ciências Sociais*' ('Social Sciences Review'), which, despite its interdisciplinary designation, specializes in publishing articles and reviews on sociology. Curiously, the first (and only) undergraduate degree in sociology was created in 1986 not by José Madureira Pinto at the Economics Faculty, but in the Classics Faculty. Pinto and his group's most distinctive contribution to sociology in Portugal came in the form of both sociological studies of Portuguese society and of epistemological writings on the conditions of production of sociological knowledge (e.g. Silva and Pinto 1986). The latter, reflecting sociology's contested status in Portuguese academia in the 1970s and 1980s, shares the same modernist and rationalist tenets of ISCTE and ICS (Nunes 1982; Almeida and Pinto 1976, 1986). The cleavage separating this modernist pole from the postmodernist Coimbra cluster of Boaventura de Sousa Santos is perhaps the most durable and significant distinction in Portuguese sociology. This is partly due to the fact that this distinction has been activated by means of intellectual interventions whereby protagonists from both poles position themselves vis-à-vis this issue (e.g. Pinto 1994: 36–37, 2007), and partly owing to the relatively minor status of the historical-comparative strand of sociology in Portugal.

Hence we come to the role of ideas and instruments in sociology in Portugal in this period. The institutionalization of sociology that took place between 1975 and 1982 drew upon theoretical and political ideas which were on the whole imported from contemporary foreign sources. It was by reference to the postmodernist turn of the late 1970s and the modernist syntheses of Bourdieu (e.g. Pinto and Pereira 2007) and Giddens' ideas, which arguably dominate the intellectual international scene, that sociologists working in Portugal at the time defined their sociological projects. The basic orientation was towards contemporary theories, methodologies, and debates, not national historical ones as suggested by continuist interpretations. In fact, there is virtually no reference to past sociological works except for those undertaken by Sedas Nunes and his cluster in the 1960s. On the contrary, from the mid-1970s onwards Portuguese sociologists elaborated Sedas Nunes' project of studying Portuguese society using theoretical and methodological lenses not that different from those of their colleagues in France and the rest of Western Europe.

What is distinctive about sociologists in Portugal in this period is the rare historical juncture afforded by a political regime change associated with a social revolution. This fact provided Portuguese sociologists with the opportunity and the challenge of creating the institutional

DOI: 10.1057/9781137495518.0004

basis upon which sociology was to develop in the following decades. In fact, in terms of both ideas and institutions, the basic framework was defined in this period. The most important departments and research centres, as well as the most significant sociological approaches, were all defined in the aftermath of 25 April 1974. Likewise, from the perspective of sociological ideas, there was very little retrospective thinking on the part of Portuguese sociologists during this period. The contrast with American sociology may put this in perspective. In the late 1960s and early 1970s, Anglo-Saxon, in particular American sociology, dedicated some of its energies to canon-formation as a way to complete and consolidate the second wave of institutionalization that had begun in 1945. Owing to the global reach of American sociology, this canon soon became canonical in other parts of the world too. The 'canonical set' (Levine 1996) Weber-Durkheim-Marx dates from the late 1960s and early 1970s.[2] While American sociologists in this period looked to the past with a view to better legitimize themselves in the present, as well as propose future avenues of research, their Portuguese counterparts were busy creating departments, undergraduate syllabi, and obtaining their own graduate training. For that, they looked not towards the past, but to the more advanced, established, and differentiated social theoretical and methodological sources of the time. As noted in the introduction, the preoccupation with sociology's lineage and genealogies in Portugal occurred decades later, either through interventions of memorialization by the first generation of Portuguese sociologists, or by historiographical studies undertaken by second-generation practitioners.

As to the instruments mobilized by sociologists to conduct their empirical work, there is little doubt that opinion surveys occupy a central place. As is well-known, surveys were first developed as methodological tools for the social sciences in the mid-1930s in the United States by the journalist-cum-pollster George Gallup and subsequently in France by Jean Stoetzel in 1938 (see Marcel 1998, 2002; Antoine 2005). Apart from some early Church surveys, in Portugal their systematic use as sociological instruments of research began only after the democratic transition. Unlike in the US and France, where surveys rapidly became a powerful symbol of positivist individualistic research programmes, enabling their practitioners to distinguish their modes of sociological inquiry from more hermeneutic and collectivist ones (Stoetzel's lifelong anti-Durkheimianism was legendary), in Portugal the minute size of the sociological community in the 1970s rendered such disciplinary differentiation strategies utterly untenable. On the contrary,

DOI: 10.1057/9781137495518.0004

what we find is an epistemologically conscious attempt to bridge the divide between quantitative and qualitative methodologies. A case in point is the use of a survey in the three-year collaborative study by Ferreira de Almeida (1986) and José Madureira Pinto (1985) of the Northwestern Portuguese village of Fonte Arcada in the late 1970s. The sociological study of Fonte Arcada inspired a number of similar case studies of local communities in the following decades, often including (as in the original study) the combination of surveys with interviews and participant observation. The mobilization of this sort of instrument expresses a fundamental theoretical-methodological orientation towards the description and analysis of Portuguese post-revolutionary society: the typical modernist class approach, which gives analytical priority to socio-economic factors as the explanatory variables of social practices and representations of a segment of a developing society in transition to democratic rule and a free market economy. Whilst culture is never given analytical priority, social practices and representations' feedback loops upon the socio-economic structure are given consideration. This research project gave rise to the first doctoral dissertations conferred by a Portuguese university, in this case ISCTE. They were José Madureira Pinto's 'Social structures and symbolic-ideological practices in the countryside: Elements of theory and empirical research' (1983),[3] and Ferreira de Almeida's 'Social classes in the countryside: Part-time peasants in a Northwestern region' (1984).[4] (see Pinto and Queirós 2010 in which this community is revisited 30 years later).

Another important instrument for sociologists is a specialized library. Again, with the partial exception of Sedas Nunes' personal library (today integrated as a collection in the library of the Institute of Social Sciences), from 1974 social sciences libraries began to be systematically created and run to support the teaching and research activities in the departments identified above. The earliest ones are the libraries of ISCTE, ICS, and the FCSH of the New University, which have been developed as generalist social science libraries. Over the years, a number of special collections have been added to their stocks (e.g. Cardoso 2013). Unsurprisingly, these libraries came to reflect in their specialization the general theoretical-methodological tenets of research units they served. Created in 1998, Coimbra's Biblioteca Norte-Sul of CES ('North-South Library') offers monographs and periodicals produced by countries from the Global South in the area of the social and human sciences, generally unavailable in Western institutions, as well as works on the Global South produced in Western countries.

DOI: 10.1057/9781137495518.0004

Academic publishers specializing in monographs in the social sciences are an important institutional outlet in the process of developing an academic discipline. As sociology began to become institutionalized in the mid-1970s, so publishers began adding to their collections book series specializing in this new discipline. In 1977 in Oporto the publisher Afrontamento published the 'Biblioteca de Ciências Sociais', the longest-running social sciences book series in Portugal. As we shall see in the next chapter, this book series would provide a crucial institutional outlet for the dissemination of sociological research outputs throughout the successive stages of disciplinary development of sociology in Portugal.

In 1982 the military tutelage that Portuguese democracy had been subjected to since the military coup of 1974 came to an end. Likewise, the early 1980s signalled the beginning of a definite turn towards European integration that would eventually lead in 1985 to Portugal joining the European Economic Community (EEC), as well as towards the blueprint of institutional modernization provided by Western democracies, including a social welfare model. As the 'rules of the game' established by the Constitution and the party system expressed not the political compromise that would pave the way for representative democracy but the leftist radicalism of the revolution, so Portuguese political culture remained squeezed into the left-hand pole of the ideological spectrum, with few structural opportunities for right-wing conservative ideological response. As we shall see, sociology in Portugal thrived under this leftist normative and institutional arrangement as it entered a new phase of development, that is, its consolidation as an academic discipline among the other social and human sciences.

Notes

1   Also in 1979, a sociology undergraduate degree was created at the University of Évora.
2   This canonical understanding of sociology's past is hugely indebted to Giddens (1971, 1976) and Alexander (1987).
3   See Pinto (1984) for the text that served as an addendum to the doctoral dissertation.
4   A complete listing of doctoral dissertations awarded by ISCTE is available online: http://iscte-iul.pt/Libraries/Listagens_teses_SID/s_doutoramento.sflb.ashx

DOI: 10.1057/9781137495518.0004

3
Consolidation, 1980s–90s

Abstract: *This is the period of consolidation of sociology as an academic discipline, marked by gradual yet salient differentiation. New specialisms emerged, a professional association was created, and various degrees in sociology were offered in universities across Portugal. Research interests generally focused upon Portuguese society, often in comparison with European cases. Two sociology journals were created during this period, one in Lisbon – Sociologia-Problemas e Práticas (1986), the other in Porto – Sociologia (1991). The first doctorates in sociology were awarded in this period. Essentially an era of institutional consolidation, the 1980s and 1990s marked a transition development stage to the present era.*

Carreira da Silva, Filipe. *Sociology in Portugal: A Short History*. Basingstoke: Palgrave Macmillan, 2016. DOI: 10.1057/9781137495518.0005.

In an essay originally delivered as a talk in September 1980 on the occasion of the award of the Theodor W. Adorno Prize by the city of Frankfurt, the German philosopher and critical theorist Jürgen Habermas introduced the idea of modernity as an 'unfinished project'. The project of modernity, following Weber, consisted in the separation of the spheres of science, morality, and art and its correspondent question of knowledge (truth), justice, and morality (normative rightness), and taste (authenticity and beauty). However, by the 1970s, the optimism that mobilized Enlightenment thinkers to imagine modernity as a project leading progressively to objective science, universal morality and law, and autonomous art was shattered (Habermas 1997: 45). Habermas' identification of the three conservatisms: (young conservatives such as Foucault or Derrida; old conservatives, epitomized by Leo Strauss, and new conservatives, who dispense traditions from any need for rational justification) opens the space for Habermas' positioning in the debate between modernist and postmodernist approaches. His intellectual intervention came in the form of a staunch defence of the Enlightenment project articulated as a general treatise in social theory – the monumental two-volume *The Theory of Communicative Action* ([1981] 1984). Apart from drawing upon little-known philosophical traditions such as American pragmatism (Silva 2006, 2007), Habermas' intellectual intervention in the debate between modernism and postmodernism clarifies the terms of the debate that was taking place in Portugal at the time. Indeed, we find an echo of that intervention in that the Habermasian terminology of modernity as an 'unfinished project', arguably with a different scope and meaning, will come to have a prominent role in the debate about the modernization of Portuguese society in the 1980s. In this debate, 'unfinished modernity' is a sociological middle-range theory of class aimed at describing the relatively late and convoluted process of socio-economic development of Portuguese society vis-à-vis comparable Western European countries (Costa and Machado 1998). Again, this modernist sociological understanding of Portugal contrasts heavily with the critical approach adopted at Coimbra, which draws upon Immanuel Wallerstein's world-system theory to depict Portugal as a 'semi-peripheral society', within a neo-Marxist account of the Portuguese state as a specific form of state domination (Santos 1985). At this point, Santos is still operating within neo-Marxism. The turn to a more resolute postmodern orientation – Habermas' first type of conservatism – occurred in the late 1980s.

DOI: 10.1057/9781137495518.0005

The context of the 1980s is also characterized by an increasing scepticism towards the social sciences, with a corresponding decrease of state funding. In the US the Reagan administration cut government funding as the social sciences become associated with 'socialism' and social engineering solutions. A similar development occurred in the United Kingdom during the Thatcher years, with sociology being out of favour for most of the 1980s. In this sense, the crisis of the welfare state was also the crisis of the social sciences. Whilst the economic and political context could hardly have been more different from the Anglo-Saxon political experiments with neo-liberalism, in Portugal there was also an apparent generalized sense of crisis in the social sciences. The focus, however, was on the consequences for the professionalization of sociologists.

Partly as a response to this challenge, a new type of agent emerged – professional associations. The Portuguese Association of Sociology (APS) was set up in 1985 and in the following year the short-lived Professional Association of Portuguese Sociologists appeared, and would play an important yet brief role in discussing sociologists' career options. The first congress of the APS took place in 1988 in the Calouste Gulbenkian Foundation under the theme 'Sociology and Portuguese Society at the Turn of the Century'. The congress focussed upon Portuguese society from a 'sociology of development' perspective, with most papers tackling the local dynamics of social change. The inaugural address was given by the ISCTE-based João Ferreira de Almeida (1988). In a paper on the professionalization dilemmas of Portuguese sociologists, António Firmino da Costa frames his argument in a specific periodization of the discipline. Besides a pre-1974 'pioneers' phase, Costa distinguishes an earlier stage of 'institutionalization' until the early 1980s and a new phase marked by the consolidation of the discipline, with a whole new set of challenges of which the professionalization of sociologists is perhaps the most urgent (Costa 1988: 118). This is very much in line with my own understanding in this volume. The topics discussed at that congress and the following one in 1992 provide a good illustration of the sociological research being undertaken in Portugal at this period. In 1988, 73 papers were presented and the four most popular topics included the sociology of knowledge and culture, urban and rural sociology, sociology of family, and sociology of work. In 1992 the number of papers presented increased to 129 and most of them focussed upon social change, education and work, and local and regional dynamics (Pinto 2004: 18). Unsurprisingly, the first wave of sociological research papers is, by and large, on Portuguese

DOI: 10.1057/9781137495518.0005

society. Their thematic orientation reveals a disciplinary concern with trying to come to terms with the nature, scope, and implications of the process of modernization in a country which had been under a right-wing dictatorship for almost half a century, had undergone a leftist revolutionary transition to democracy in the previous decade, and was now reorienting itself for the first time towards Western Europe rather than the Atlantic and the colonial empire.

What a discipline studies reveals as much about it as what is left unsaid (or silenced). One of the great 'silences' in these first congresses, and indeed in sociology in Portugal since its inception generally, is the colonial empire. Not that it was ever possible to fully explain and understand Portuguese society without a reference to the colonial empire that stretched over Austral Africa (Angola and Mozambique), the Western seaboard of India (namely, Goa), into South East Asia (Macao and East-Timor). Until 1974 Portuguese society encompassed these colonial territories in both a juridical-political and an identity sense. After 1974, the process of decolonization, which involved the rushed immigration of hundreds of thousands of 'retornados' ('returnees'; what the French would call 'Pieds-Noirs'), plunging the newly independent countries into civil wars that lasted well into the 1990s, has been perhaps the most convoluted collective experience in democratic Portugal. The fact remains that, both before and since 1974, any project referring to a sociology *of* Portugal is radically incomplete without reference to the colonial empire (however, see Pires 1984 and his interview in Chapter 5) and the 'cultural trauma' (e.g. Alexander et al. 2004) associated with it – either in the sense of a collective loss by the more conservative segments of Portuguese society, or in the sense of a collective process of acknowledging and repairing the horrors of colonial rule.

If before 1974 there were political reasons for this silence, the reasons for maintaining this silence afterwards are more complex. Despite the constant self-congratulatory claims about self-reflexivity, sociology's inability to address this central feature of Portuguese society reiterates, rather than questions, that society's difficulties in dealing with this experience. As in the case of other former colonial powers, there are theoretical and political reasons for this blind spot. Modernist approaches typically equate society, as sociology's central analytical category, with the nation-state. The notion of a transcontinental imperial society, even if existing only in collective memory, fits uneasily with such a methodological nationalism. Politically, as other similar cases show, the ways in which

DOI: 10.1057/9781137495518.0005

Western democracies negotiate their postcolonial status, that is, the kind of diplomatic and economic ties they establish with former colonies, the way they treat emigrants from those countries, organize school curricula regarding that historical period, deal with memorializing monuments and events, and so on, is sensitive to say the least. Sociology in the 1980s, however, was exceptionally well equipped to address colonial experiences, dynamics, and mechanisms. Arguably, S.N. Eisenstadt's structuralist-functionalist political sociology of empires (1963) was irremediably outdated by the 1980s. In the wake of Edward Said's culturalist construction of 'orientalism' (1979), the 1980s witnessed a revolution in the study of former colonial empires. The focus was no longer upon accounting for their institutional features, but upon exposing the underlying structures of domination that regulate the transnational circulation of objects, people, and ideas. The emphasis on migratory flows as constitutive of collective experiences in postcolonial studies is well illustrated by the work of British sociologist Paul Gilroy. Gilroy's path-breaking study *The Black Atlantic* (1993), at the centre of which one finds a culturalist rendering of Du Bois' concept of 'double consciousness' (Reed 1997), points to the culturally constructed nature of African intellectual history as both European and black, crucial to which were the travels of many African-American writers in a transatlantic context. The Atlantic emerges from Gilroy's analysis as a space of transnational cultural construction, which forces us – Europeans and Africans, or both – to look beyond the confines of cultural nationalism. In rigour, Gilroy's 1993 study was but one application of the much broader cultural studies approach developed by the famous Birmingham Centre for Contemporary Cultural Studies (CCCS) since the 1960s (e.g. Hoggarth 1957; Gilroy et al. 1982; see also Hall 1992). By contrast, at this stage, Portuguese sociologists were either uninterested in looking back at their uncomfortable colonial experience (the present and future were now decidedly European), or most of them utilized modernist materialist approaches which prevented them from analysing their own colonial past as a transnational cultural construction – simultaneously European and African. As we shall see in the next chapter, the challenge to take up this study will be (partially) met only into the 1990s by the Coimbra school, at which time both the theoretical and political conditions were met.

Another glaring absence, contrary to what might be expected, is the almost total lack of dialogue and collaboration with Brazilian sociology. Cultural and linguistic ties definitely did not suffice to make Brazil a comparable influence upon Western sociological sources in the

DOI: 10.1057/9781137495518.0005

establishment of sociology in Portugal, apart from the occasional foot-note (e.g. Nunes 1965: 9). It is as if one could conceive of British sociology being developed in the post-war period with no reference to what was going on in sociology departments in the US. But the fact is that, by and large, sociology in Portugal in the 1980s and 1990s consolidated itself under no significant influence from Brazilian sociology, despite the latter's international renown and wealth of empirical analysis. This situation would change only with the establishment of the Luso-Afro-Brazilian Congress, one of the world's few intercontinental networks of academic conferences in the social sciences. The first event was organized by Coimbra's CES in 1990 and it has been taking place every two years ever since in social science departments or research centres in Europe, Africa, and America. In reality, however, even this institutional platform of collaboration has done relatively little to shape the minute exchange of ideas between sociology in Brazil and sociology in Portugal.

Another key idea the sociological treatment of which sheds light upon the dynamics of the discipline is the concept of the state. In the 1980s and 1990s, the state still figured centrally in many sociological pieces by Portuguese practitioners. Santos' aforementioned analysis of Portuguese society in the mid-1980s is, in effect, a sociological analysis of the Portuguese state. Whilst sociologists' gaze focused largely upon social agents and on the structure that frames their conduct and beliefs, there was still the generalized sense that Portuguese society could not possibly be studied without reference to the state. This would gradually cease to be the case in the 1990s. The reason for this was the process of differentiation of academic disciplines within Portuguese academia. By the time political science in Portugal was established as an independent discipline, sociology was already itself a consolidated discipline. The first undergraduate degree dates from 1996 (at the New University), and the Portuguese Association of Political Science was created three years later in 1999. But the institutionalization of political science in Portugal was exceptionally successful. Within a decade, a number of university undergraduate and graduate programmes were created, following the American four-part model of national politics, comparative politics, international relations, and political theory (on the 'Americanization' of political science in Portugal, see e.g. Pinto 2011: 609). With the creation and institutionalization of political science, the notion of the 'state' with-ered from sociology's agenda. Once a popular sociological specialism, political sociology soon became a minor teaching and research outlet.

DOI: 10.1057/9781137495518.0005

In short, the history of sociology in Portugal cannot be analysed without reference to the wider system of academic disciplines to which it belongs, most proximately the social sciences, but also the Portuguese university system as a whole.

The consolidation of sociology as an academic discipline reveals itself in the sort of instruments mobilized by sociologists. The main instrument remains, by and large, the survey of reported opinions and practices. In the 1980s and early 1990s, a growing number of surveys were applied to the study of segments of Portuguese society, often in conjunction with such qualitative methodological instruments as in-depth interviews. In addition, official statistics were increasingly used as a means of describing social realities. The intended result was a more detailed and quantifiable depiction of the national social structure and certain dynamics of social change (for instance, in terms of values, see Almeida and Costa 1990). Let me briefly illustrate my argument with two concrete examples. In 1985 *Análise Social* published a three-volume special issue entitled 'Social Changes in Contemporary Portugal' (1985: issues 87–89). The contents of this special issue originated in a workshop held at the Institute of Social Sciences of the University of Lisbon, the institutional successor of the original GIS. This workshop was one of four held in the academic year 1984–85 on youth and religion, women, and cooperation with African Portuguese-speaking countries. Only the papers presented in the workshop on social change, however, were published in the journal. The special issue reflects well the main disciplinary trends in Portugal in the 1980s. Six parts, each including four articles, cover economic life, the class structure, political organizations and movements, the Portuguese state, family and demography, and education. The overall focus is upon national institutions, processes of change, social agents, and ideologies. Statistics and surveys are the privileged instruments of research. Fittingly, the cover of the special issue figures an image of the Portuguese territory, criss-crossed with colourful stripes suggesting lines of communication of goods, people, and ideas within the national borders. In an important sense, then, this special issue coordinated by Sedas Nunes mirrored the special issues that had made the reputation of *Análise Social* in the mid-1960s. The main differences, of course, were the (wider) breadth of topics and the presence of a relatively large number of participants whose main training was in sociology. But the same modernist aim of providing the state administration and the public in general with quantifiable sociological knowledge remains central.

DOI: 10.1057/9781137495518.0005

The second example I wish to discuss is from a decade later. In 1996 ICS-based António Barreto edited a collaborative report funded by the Tinker Foundation, an American foundation whose geo-cultural focus is Iberia and Latin America, on Portugal's social condition between 1960 and 1995 (Barreto 1996). Pre-published in part in a daily newspaper and a media sensation at the time, this report distinguishes itself by the extensive usage of statistics to factually describe as accurately and comprehensively as possible the main dimensions of Portuguese social structure: general patterns of social change (population, health care, etc.); demographic trends; ageing; mores; the economy; and social welfare policies. A typical example of the use of statistics by social scientists both to provide authorities with reliable social knowledge and to self-legitimize sociology as the main institutional producer of such statistics, the publication of this report, alongside other collective volumes on Portuguese society by ISCTE (Viegas and Costa 1998) and CES (Santos 1993) can be said to signal the consolidation of sociology in Portugal.

Towards the end of this phase of consolidation a new development occurred which would have ample consequences for the future of the discipline in Portugal. I refer to the accession of Portuguese research organizations to international networks aimed at producing comparable cross-national and longitudinal attitudinal data. The first international surveys of social attitudes and practices appeared as sociology in Portugal was in the process of being institutionalized and developed as it consolidated itself in the following decades. Concretely, my point is that the development of international surveys not only contributed to the consolidation of sociology in Portugal, but would also eventually lead to its internationalization. The history of this instrument of research and of the institutional outlets of collaboration around it, in other words, sheds important light upon successive stages of disciplinary development of sociology in the country.

Benefiting from the collaboration of Ronald Inglehart, who was then developing a theory accounting for the change from materialist to post-materialist values in developed societies (Inglehart 1977), the Eurobarometer was launched in the early 1970s as a bi-annual public opin-ion survey in all member states of the then Common Market on behalf of the European Commission. Another early international survey was the European Values Study (EVS). First applied in 1981 in the contemporary EU Member States, as well as the US and Canada, the EVS was set up to study the basic human values underlying European social and political

DOI: 10.1057/9781137495518.0005

institutions.[1] In 1984 the International Social Sciences Programme (ISSP) was created. The focus of the ISSP was not merely European but global. Its aim was to run periodical surveys on topics important for the social sciences, with each national member being responsible for funding and applying its own survey. In 2001 the European Social Survey (ESS) was created with the aim of providing complementary data on European public opinion on a variety of issues of political and economic import. With Spain, Portugal began to apply the Eurobarometer upon its integration in the then EEC in 1985. From 1990, Portugal has participated in the three last waves of the EVS.[2] Portugal first joined the ISSP in the 1997 round on 'Work Orientations II'. Portugal has been a national member of the ESS since the beginning. The national representative of both the ISSP and the ESS is the Institute of Social Sciences of the University of Lisbon. As we shall see in the next chapter, this institutional affiliation would have important editorial consequences.

In the mid-1970s there were no specialized academic publishers in the social sciences in Portugal. By the 1990s, however, there were several. In less than 20 years, some of these publishers had assembled a catalogue with dozens of titles, including translations of important theoretical and methodological works. As institutional outlets connecting research outputs and the reading public, academic publishers performed a crucial function in the consolidation of sociology in the 1980s and 1990s. A case in point is Oporto-based Afrontamento, whose social sciences series ('Biblioteca de Ciências Sociais') includes a sociology subsection with almost 100 titles.[3] The development of this historic book series provides a useful insight into the very development of the research interests of sociologists based in Oporto and Coimbra. Three periods are discernible. There is an early phase when case studies and introductory methodological and epistemological writings predominate (including a three-volume commentary on Marx), a subsequent phase focussing upon the modernism vs. postmodernism debate of the 1980s, and a more recent phase with a much more differentiated sociological production, including works in translation. As we shall see, this change in editorial output reflected a new stage in the development of this academic discipline. Down in Lisbon, there are two main academic publishers with a significant sociology specialization. One was Celta, a publisher based at ISCTE. A product of a consolidated discipline, Celta was created in 1992 to respond to the need for an institutionalized publishing outlet for the growing sociological output of ISCTE sociologists, as well as for

DOI: 10.1057/9781137495518.0005

the publication of crucial works in translation (Bourdieu and Giddens are the most translated authors). At ICS, António Barreto led a similar development. Between the 1970s and early 1990s, the publication of works by sociologists and other social scientists based at ICS had been undertaken on a case-by-case basis, often in collaboration with commercial publishers. By the mid-1990s, there were signs that this situation was no longer feasible and a more institutionalized outlet was needed. As a result, in 1998 the 'Imprensa de Ciências Sociais' (ICS), its acronym identical to the Institute's, was created for the purpose of divulging the social-scientific production of the ICS. An interdisciplinary publisher in the social sciences, ICS has a 'sociology' book series with over 100 titles. Unlike other academic publishers, ICS does not publish translations of sociological texts.[4] These developments in Portugal's academic book trade, along with several specialized book series by commercial publishers, constitute yet another sign of the consolidation of sociology in Portugal.

Alongside academic publishers, as an institutional outlet, journals perform an important function in the process of consolidation of an academic discipline. Until the early 1980s, there were only two main sociology journals in the country – *Análise Social* and *Revista Crítica de Ciências Sociais* – even though these have always been interdisciplinary journals. This was soon to change. In less than a decade, twice as many new sociology journals were appearing. As noted, in 1984 '*Cadernos de Ciências Sociais*' appeared from the Economics Faculty of the University of Porto. In 1986 the sociology department of ISCTE launched '*Sociologia – Problemas e Práticas*'. This is, in effect, the first specialized scientific journal in sociology in Portugal. In 1991 the Institute of Sociology in the Classics Faculty of the University of Porto (IS-FLUP) published '*Sociologia*'. In the following year, yet another sociology journal appeared, this time in Lisbon. Moisés Espírito Santo, a sociologist of religion based at the Human and Social Sciences Faculty of the New University founded '*Fórum Sociológico*' in 1992. This would be short-lived, however. In 1995 *Fórum Sociológico* was discontinued. With a new editorial team, a second series of the journal has been running since 1999.[5] This proliferation of scientific journals is an indisputable sign of the consolidation of sociology in Portugal. With the exponential increase in sociological outputs, the nascent Portuguese sociological community followed in the wake of other established epistemic communities and organized institutional outlets for the dissemination of its findings. Of course, journals also

DOI: 10.1057/9781137495518.0005

provide agents with institutionalized outlets for positioning themselves in the field vis-à-vis other agents and the general reading public through intellectual interventions. In this sense, the publication profile of each of these journals reveals a specific theoretical-methodological orientation, the evolution of which often follows larger developments in that specific community and/or in the discipline as a whole. As these developments suggest, the phase of consolidation is also characterized by another fact. For the most part, sociologists in Portugal focus upon Portuguese social realities and publish their findings in local journals. This too was about to change.

No discipline is able to consolidate itself in an environment as competitive as the higher education system without solid teaching institutions. As in the case of journals, the 1980s and 1990s were characterized by the rapid proliferation of undergraduate degrees in sociology. Six new undergraduate degrees were established in public universities between 1985 and 1994. Masters degrees in sociology followed rapidly. In 1984 the first MPhil in sociology was offered by the New University of Lisbon, followed by another at ISCTE in 1989. Doctoral degrees, however, are still few and far between. The first doctoral programmes in sociology only appeared in the 2000s. Given the late institutionalization of sociology in Portugal, Portuguese sociologists either obtained their degrees from foreign universities or did ad-hoc PhDs in their own time. In fact, until well into the 1980s, the vast majority of Portuguese sociologists obtained their doctorates abroad. Once again, the absence of collaboration with Brazilian academia is glaring. Contrary to what might have been expected given the cultural and linguistic ties with the ex-colony, and despite Brazil having had graduate programmes in sociology running since the late 1960s, all of these early doctorates were obtained in Western countries. It is only from the mid-1980s that Portuguese sociologists began obtaining their doctorates at home institutions. Whilst minute, the rapid progression in figures is impressive. Between 1974 and 1979, six doctorates in sociology were officially recognized by Portuguese universities. Including doctorates obtained abroad and in Portugal, between 1980 and 1989 that figure rose to 49, and between 1990 and 1999 there were 144 new doctors in sociology (Machado 2009: 292).

The problem facing the Portuguese sociological community in the 1980s and 1990s was that of consolidating the institutionalization of sociology within the country's university system. By the early 1990s, that challenge had been overcome. Despite its blind spots, sociology

DOI: 10.1057/9781137495518.0005

in Portugal developed in the main as a sociology *of* Portugal along two principal and opposing theoretical-methodological programmes within an expanding institutional framework with new publication outlets and an increasing number of sociology departments and research centres.

Notes

1   http://www.europeanvaluesstudy.eu/frmShowpage?v_page_id=4494595474065608
The EVS has carried out three subsequent waves in 1990, 1999–2000, and 2008.

2   https://dbk.gesis.org/dbksearch/file.asp?file=ZA4804_EVS_ParticipatingCountries.pdf

3   http://www.edicoesafrontamento.pt/cataacutelogo.html

4   https://www.imprensa.ics.ulisboa.pt/

5   http://cesnova.fcsh.unl.pt/?area=000&mid=005&id=PUB4de4bd06d1a0f

DOI: 10.1057/9781137495518.0005

4

Internationalization, 1995 to the Present Day

Abstract: *This chapter discusses the current phase of development of sociology in Portugal as one characterized by internationalization. Internationalization is here understood to refer both to a stage of development and to the challenge involved in making use of key sociological ideas and instruments within a changing institutional setting. Unlike the phases previously discussed, internationalization is a global phenomenon that has impacted sociology in Portugal from abroad. Hence, while most of the challenges discussed here are common to other national sociologies, the responses that Portuguese sociologists and institutions have articulated are relatively specific. One outstanding feature is the expanded notion of Portuguese society that sociologists have been elaborating since the 1990s. If nowadays 'societies' are less and less equated with 'territorial nation-states', in the Portuguese case, as in other post-imperial Western countries, this has entailed a critical re-examination of the (culturally traumatic) colonial experience.*

Carreira da Silva, Filipe. *Sociology in Portugal: A Short History*. Basingstoke: Palgrave Macmillan, 2016. DOI: 10.1057/9781137495518.0006.

The early 1990s mark the end of the Cold War. The fall of the Berlin Wall in 1989, the collapse of the Soviet Union in 1991, and the end of the Apartheid regime in South Africa in 1994 signal the end of the historical era that had begun in 1945 (or, indeed, a century before; see Hobsbawn 1994), and the dawn of a new historical period marked by the challenges of globalization. Confirming some of the prognoses of postmodernism (Lyotard 1979: 3–6), the rapid expansion of the Internet, the World Wide Web, and a host of new information technologies after the mid-1990s only accelerated this societal shift. For a brief moment, there were those who suggested that the shift signalled the 'end of history' and the irreversible victory of free market economics and liberal democracy, but this idea soon proved to be a myth. If anything, nationalism, religion, cultural wars, and identity politics have commanded much of our attention since then. One thing seems certain, however. Solid and entrenched industrial modernity is no more. This new era has been accompanied by a change in fundamental institutional forms associated with industrial class-based modernity. Science today is increasingly organized and performed through inter- and sometimes transdisciplinary projects and networks (Nowotny, Scott, and Gibbons 2001). At a political level, a similar retreat from the modern institutional political form par excellence, the territorial nation-state, has been subject to detailed scrutiny for at least a generation. The challenge confronting us today is that these two modern institutional forms, academic disciplines and nation-states, no longer enjoy the overwhelming dominance that they possessed for most of the last two centuries, especially in Western Europe and the US. This recognition frames the topic of this chapter, that is, how collective and individual agents have coped with the new phase and challenge of internationalization, and, in turn, how their responses have helped reshape sociology in Portugal. Before I discuss internationalization, let me briefly analyse the current challenges facing academic disciplines and nation-states.

Much of contemporary social theory has been developed with the aim of understanding the nature and implications of this epochal shift for both disciplines, namely in the social sciences, and for nation-states. In Portugal, this shift was interpreted less in terms of Habermas' thesis of the unfinished project of modernity, or the (self-defeating) postmodernist narrative of the end of modernity, than according to the Beck-Giddens-Lash 'reflexive modernization' approach (1994). The Eurocentric character of this approach, however, was largely overlooked by the Portuguese

DOI: 10.1057/9781137495518.0006

sociological community which found in it a useful toolkit with which to undertake empirical research.[1] Partly owing to its provincial character, this approach has been largely abandoned today. In the work of Shmuel N. Eisenstadt and his associates one finds a much more comprehensive and theoretically consistent approach. Their basic idea is that conceiving of *multiple modernities* is a more convincing way of coping with the irreducible differences between different civilizational interpretations of the modern programme (Eisenstadt 2002, 2003). As I have argued elsewhere (Silva 2008: 9–30), I am of the view that Eisenstadt's paradigm is a refreshing and important corrective to the ubiquitous equation of Europeanization with modernization. Yet I am not convinced that there is sufficient empirical evidence to back the thesis of completely autonomous modernities, in the sense of separate civilizational units in which independent processes of modernization emerge and unfold. I am equally sceptical, however, of accounts of neo-modernization. A case in point is Volker Schmidt's neo-Parsonian concept of a 'global modernity' (2014; see also 2006, 2007), according to which the process of functional differentiation still constitutes the best analytical reference to explain the diffusion of modernity. As I will attempt to show in this chapter by reference to the Portuguese case, other patterns besides differentiation can be seen to operate in the realms of science and democratic politics. I view both the multiple modernities proposal and neo-modernization theories as unsatisfactory responses to the question of how to conceive of modernity today. Rather, my alternative points towards a plural modernity, with several organizing societal patterns operating in various institutional realms in different regional sub-units that may, following Peter A. Hall's 'varieties of capitalism' (Hall and Soskice 2001), be designated as 'varieties of modernity'.

As several authors have pointed out, after an initial phase in which interdisciplinarity marked the beginning of the end of the hegemonic reign of disciplines as self-enclosed organizational units, scientific practice today is increasingly dominated by transdisciplinary endeavours (Klein 1990). From research projects that bring together numerous practitioners in different fields to resolve a given problem, to large international networks of scientists collaborating in postgraduate programmes and research and development initiatives, the scientific landscape today is no longer dominated by academic disciplines. In my view, however, one should be careful not to dismiss too readily the organizational function performed by disciplines. Ours may no longer be a 'disciplinary age' per se, but the

DOI: 10.1057/9781137495518.0006

emerging 'post-disciplinary' era certainly does not preclude a central role for this specific institutional form. In order to understand why I believe this to be so, a few comments on the chief organizational patterns of the contemporary academic system may be in order.

There are two main methodological and theoretical orientations that can be observed in modern academia (Heilbron 2004). First, there are those who favour a systems theoretical perspective. Their main influence is Reinhart Koselleck, for whom a major societal break occurred between 1750 and 1850. The modern understanding of the term 'discipline' was born in this epoch and expressed a structural transformation of higher learning. These authors claim that the modern academic system is but a subsystem of the social system and is subject to the very same functional requirements and organizational patterns. Disciplines are, from this viewpoint, the main institutional form brought about by modernity, one that came to replace the older, less professionalized clubs, salons, and learned societies. Secondly, the work of Michel Foucault provides an alternative perspective to the systems theory. Drawing upon the French tradition of historical epistemology (in particular, the work of Bachelard and Canguilhem), Foucault ([1966] 1970) identifies an epistemological break marking the emergence of the modern era. But this epistemological break was not a purely discursive phenomenon. A new institutional form emerged as a correlate of this rupture. Disciplines were born, and through them modern science acquired an extremely efficient institutional structure that enabled pursuit of the modern project of control to previously unimaginable levels (Foucault [1975] (1991).

In recent years, both of these perspectives have been subject to severe criticism. In particular, the image of a sudden break at the end of the eighteenth century, inaugurating an ever more homogeneous yet differentiated modernity, lacks empirical sustainability. The image of modernity as an ever more coherent monolith underlying the work of both Foucault and the system theorists can be criticized for its fetishized character. In particular, and contrary to what the latter suggest, there is simply no empirical indication that the European academic system was institutionally less heterogeneous before 1800 than afterwards. If anything, the opposite seems to be true (Heilbron 2004: 28–29). Furthermore, the history of modern science has plenty of examples of disciplines that evolved according to developmental patterns other than differentiation. Biology is a well-known example of a discipline formed via the logic of synthesis, integrating a number of previously separate

DOI: 10.1057/9781137495518.0006

domains (botany, zoology, medicine, etc.) into a new and more general science of life. Chemistry, on the other hand, exemplifies how a craft-like practice was upgraded into a full-fledged academic discipline by applying principles of the established sciences (Heilbron 2004: 36). In short, the logic of differentiation is but one of the operating logics under modern conditions.

Furthermore, as these modern conditions have rapidly changed in recent decades, one wonders what the most adequate diagnosis of the present situation might be. As noted in the introduction, there is a growing consensus among sociologists of science that we are living in a post-disciplinary age. The general trend of erosion of disciplines as the predominant mode of organization in scientific work, deemed too bureaucratic and rigid to cope with the flexibility requirements of our globalized era, is said to be the chief trait of science during the early decades of the twenty-first century. I subscribe to most aspects of this diagnosis. Specifically, I find very plausible the claim by Michael Gibbons that transdisciplinarity is the emerging disciplinary mode. The production of knowledge is increasingly: 'oriented towards and driven by problem-solving' (Gibbons et al. 1994: 24; see also Klein et al. 2004). The production of knowledge as a means of problem-solving, rather than the production of positive facts through rational or mathematical treat-ments, is, of course, the hallmark of a pragmatic philosophy of science. Such a new mode of knowledge production is inherently performative, presupposing a permanent oscillation between the fundamental and the applied. In addition, contrary to neo-modernization models, transdisci-plinarity expresses a logic not of differentiation but of *de*-differentiation. Communicative networks between researchers have grown increasingly denser, bringing together different actors, modes of doing, and value orientations. Nevertheless, academic disciplines remain the most impor-tant institutional form of scientific activity. As the case of academic sociology in Portugal shows, the problem-solving capability envisaged by Gibbons is simply unthinkable without the training, conceptual and methodological tools, and intellectual traditions that only disciplines are able to provide and guarantee. In order to collaborate in an interdiscipli-nary or transdisciplinary project, one must be a practitioner of a certain discipline.

If, in the scientific domain, academic disciplines are the modern institutional form, the same can be said of the territorial nation-state for the political realm. It should thus not come as a surprise that strikingly

DOI: 10.1057/9781137495518.0006

similar claims are being made in these two different debates. While in debates on science we are told that we are now living in a post-disciplinary era, an increasing number of political theorists claim that the nation-state is an institutional form of a bygone era. Lurking behind these claims yet again is the work of Foucault. As he showed in the 1970s, the process of state consolidation from the seventeenth to the nineteenth centuries took place not only at the institutional level but also, and fundamentally, in the realm of political thought. The state appeared then, for the first time, as an object with measurable properties, such as its wealth and power, to be studied by political arithmetic, statistics, and political economy. By contrast, medieval and early modern political thought was primarily occupied with cities and their troubled relationship with rising states (Isin 1999: 166). This historical legacy has now been re-appropriated by much urban literature. A central difficulty with these proposals is the dismissal of the state that they presuppose. Like the dismissal of academic disciplines, it is unwarranted and premature. States continue to wield important mechanisms that contribute to the shaping of social and economic contexts within their borders.

Let me now discuss what these changes have meant for sociology in Portugal since the mid-1990s. As we have seen, between 1963 and the mid-1990s, there are three different stages of development and one defining discontinuity in the history of sociology in Portugal. But trespassing this discontinuity and uniting all these phases is one central fact: to a large extent, sociology in Portugal is a sociology *of* Portugal. This has changed since the mid-1990s, however. From that point onwards, a new phase and challenge emerged, that is, the exponential rise of the internationalization of science. In a sense, of course, science has always been international. National borders, or any kind of borders for that matter (Abbott 2001), are intrinsically inimical to the free exchange of ideas, techniques, and human agents that characterize scientific activities. Yet borders matter. They impose a certain order upon the inherent chaos of scientific inquiry, thus fostering its organization, efficiency, and efficacy. But today borders – national or disciplinary – matter less than they did a few decades ago. Science has become more internationalized as national frontiers have declined in importance. Over the last few decades, national epistemic communities have gradually become more oriented towards each other rather than around themselves. This is noticeable in every aspect of scientific activity, from how and what one studies, where one's findings are published, who funded that research, and who its addressees

DOI: 10.1057/9781137495518.0006

are. As Portuguese sociologists and institutions began to engage with this global phenomenon in the 1990s, their focus was gradually reoriented towards other epistemic communities. Rather than primarily talking among themselves, many began to address an international audience. Thematically, sociology in Portugal gradually ceased to be primarily a sociology *of* Portugal, as 'Portugal' itself become increasingly studied as a transnational, transhistorical, and transcultural entity no longer limited to the territorial boundaries of the Portuguese Republic or by a materialist conception of its social structure.

Internationalization can be interpreted as both a stage of development and a challenge to how agents in specific countries, research, or teaching institutions organize their activities. A few figures suffice to clarify the nature and extent of this phenomenon. From 1997 to 2007, the number of research scientists (excluding social sciences and humanities) increased from 5.2 million to 7.2 million. While impressive, these figures pale in comparison with the growth in global scientific outputs, including the social sciences. From 450,000 journal articles published in 1980, this figure skyrocketed to a staggering two million in 2015 and is expected to reach four million in the next decade.[2] This provides a fairly accurate measure of the growing pace of internationalization of science since the 1990s.

Yet internationalization of an academic discipline is much more than figures concerning scientific outputs or the number of research scientists. It is fundamentally about new ways of doing science. First and foremost, internationalization is about *how* one undertakes research. Collaboration with international research networks around the application of cross-national surveys have proved very important in this regard. The entanglement between ideas and instruments is often pivotal in pushing forward disciplinary modes of teaching and research. Portuguese sociologists have tried to adapt their agendas to these real-world developments and theoretical innovations. A case in point is Manuel Villaverde Cabral et al.'s (2008) comparative study of urban governance and citizen participation using survey data from the International Social Survey Programme 2004, which in the Portuguese case includes an over-represented sample of the Lisbon metropolitan area. This collected volume is part of the 'Portuguese Social Attitudes' ('Atitudes Sociais dos Portugueses') book series, which has published numerous volumes on different waves from multiple international survey programmes, from the ISSP 1997 module on work orientations (Cabral, Vala, and Freire 2000) to the ESS Round 4 2008

DOI: 10.1057/9781137495518.0006

rotating module on welfare state attitudes (Silva 2013).[3] As this example illustrates, the crisis of modernist understandings of the categories of the nation-state and academic disciplines have provided new exciting topics of research, often explored in comparison with other cases.

Internationalization is also about the *addressees* of one's research. Publishing in international academic publishers and journals allows one to reach an audience that local outlets do not. Internationalization also stimulates researchers from different countries to confront their research findings in the same journals and publishers, thus moving beyond domestic, self-enclosed, and protected circuits of publication. Moreover, since top-ranked publication outlets have stricter peer-review criteria this also means a more demanding scrutiny of one's scientific findings. Publishing in English for a global audience has become the trademark of the trend towards internationalization. As career opportunities and professional prestige became increasingly associated with the global impact of their work, Portuguese sociologists have been publishing more frequently in international journals and academic publishers. The small size of the Portuguese sociological community might have also contributed to this. In larger countries with differentiated domestic epistemic communities, such as the US and Germany, sociologists have little incentive to go beyond what is already a numerous audience. By contrast, in small countries the national community is often not large enough to provide an adequate audience for most specialisms. Small epistemic communities may work in such cases as another incentive to address an international audience through publications, conference papers, or participation in international research projects. Whatever the reasons may have been for the growing internationalization of the Portuguese sociological community in the last couple of decades, the fact is that there is growing awareness that the sociological relevance of Portuguese social and political reality is increasingly a function of its contribution to the international scholarship in each specialism. A growing number of Portuguese sociologists now seem to believe that it is not sufficient to publish locally if their findings are to be valid. True validation requires scrutiny from peers and this is not confined to local epistemic communities. The meaning of local phenomena and events emerges out of its systematic confrontation with comparable local phenomena and events in other countries in order to find general patterns and exceptions. Cases such as the 2013 special issue of *European Societies* dedicated to the theme of whether there still is a Southern European welfare regime, where an

DOI: 10.1057/9781137495518.0006

article on the Portuguese case stands side-by-side with similar case studies on Spain, Italy, and Greece as well as more general regional analyses, have become increasingly common in the last few years.[4] On the other hand, the challenge posed by internationalization has also provided a powerful stimulus for change in the governance of scientific journals based in Portugal. National journals in the social sciences have increasingly adopted international standards of blind peer-review. *Análise Social* provides a good illustration of this development. From a journal in which social-scientific findings on Portuguese society were published by the local community of social scientists in the 1960s, this journal adopts peer-review procedures in the mid-1990s, and is nowadays indexed in ISI, Scopus, and JSTOR. In 2002 a new peer-reviewed journal, published entirely in English, was created: the *Portuguese Journal of Social Science*. These developments are not substantively different from others around the world, where journals are being incentivized to adopt international standards of peer-review in order to be included in global indexes of scientific journals. Yet, taken together, these developments also mean a larger number of publication outlets and an intensification of the fluxes of international collaboration and citation. This, in my view, is the most significant trait of this institutional change.

Internationalization is also about institutions. To begin with, the institutionalization and consolidation of sociology in Portugal between the late 1960s and the 1990s is an overwhelmingly public affair. Virtually all Portuguese universities were run by the state until this time under a model similar to that of other Continental European countries, with typical long contributory careers, job security, little mobility within institutions, and high levels of inbreeding. In such a model, the professional incentives to publish in peer-reviewed journals or to get research funding from competitive foreign agencies are limited. This model, however, has been under attack by new modes of governance, including the so-called 'new public management' audit culture, and faced competition from private universities from the 2000s onwards. In this sense, the post-1990s phase is also one of massification, with a rising number of students enrolled on higher degree programmes whose quality was not always the best (Pais and Cabral 2006: 862). But it is also a phase of substantial public investment in research institutions, namely around a national network of state 'Associate Laboratories'. Two of these new institutional outlets included sociology as one of their thematic domains: the Associate Laboratory of the Institute of Social Sciences of the University of Lisbon, and the

DOI: 10.1057/9781137495518.0006

Associate Laboratory of the Centre for Social Studies at the University of Coimbra, both created in 2002.[5] These new two outlets, alongside CIES and CESNOVA but with slightly different juridical status, were pivotal in expanding and consolidating a highly internationalized younger generation of social scientists, including sociologists. Yet another institutional development in this period has been the reinforcement of the policy orientation of public universities. As a result, a number of observatories have been created in this period, covering such topics as youth (1989), justice (1996), cultural activities (1996), the environment (1996), local government (2002), education (2003), and inequality (2008). All these observatories depend upon public funding to function and, as in most other countries, are intended to provide social knowledge to improve public decision-making.

National and supranational institutions responsible for funding scientific research, namely public institutions, have performed a pivotal role in supporting and directing Portuguese sociologists to more internationalized careers. But how agents have responded to these institutional incentives has varied significantly. An often overplayed factor has to do with the theoretical orientation of one's work and its openness to interdisciplinary modes of inquiry. The case of the European Research Council (ERC), founded in 2007 and the leading supranational institution in Europe that funds basic research, helps to illustrate my point. The ERC funding scheme distinguishes their grantees on the basis of their relative position on the academic ladder. Younger researchers can apply for an ERC Starting or Consolidator Grant up until 12 years after receiving their PhD, while ERC Advanced Investigator Grants are aimed at senior researchers. Between 2007 and 2015, only three sociologists based in Portugal won ERC grants. In 2010 an Advanced ERC Grant was awarded to Boaventura Sousa Santos, whose career has had an international orientation since the 1970s. Three years later, ICS-based Sofia Aboim was awarded a Consolidator Grant and Ana Cristina Santos, a member of the Coimbra cluster, won a Starting Grant. Typical of the younger generation of Portuguese sociologists, both Aboim and Santos have pre-eminently international research profiles. The ERC funding scheme is important for my purposes for yet another reason. As Fleck and Hönig have shown, this scheme does not support established disciplines as such but rather a: 'post-disciplinary world of scholarship' (2015: 40). In this post-disciplinary context, some disciplines in the social sciences emerge as more successful than others. Certain disciplines such as economics

DOI: 10.1057/9781137495518.0006

and history have been more successful in attracting funding from this scheme, partly owing to the specific nature of the ERC panel structure. In the case of sociology, it finds itself in competition with new emerging research domains, such as urban or cultural studies (2015: 58). The three Portuguese research projects cited above illustrate well this general trend. Boaventura de Sousa Santos' ALICE aims at promoting institutional reform in Europe by learning from the experiences of five non-European countries in the fields of human rights, democracy, and social cohesion.[6] Sofia Aboim's TRANSRIGHTS undertakes a cross-national and transnational comparative analysis of the lives of trans-people in five European countries – Portugal, the United Kingdom, France, Sweden, and the Netherlands – in order to see how legal and institutional frameworks impact their lives.[7] Finally, Ana Cristina Santos' INTIMA offers a comparative qualitative study of the legal, political, and cultural context for LGBT intimate citizenship in Italy, Portugal, and Spain.[8] One reason for their success seems to have been that all three scholars combine sociological, theoretical, and methodological resources with elements from critical theory, cultural studies, and feminist thinking, with a more or less explicit activist agenda in the case of the projects originating in Coimbra. In short, coping with the challenge of internationalization also means responding to the challenges of a post-disciplinary age.

The national funding agency for scientific research, the Portuguese Foundation for Science and Technology (FCT), has embraced internationalization as a central policy principle guiding its funding priorities at least since the late 1990s.[9] Unlike the ERC, however, FCT panels for both individual scholarships (PhD and post-doctoral) and research projects follow a strictly disciplinary logic. As a result, in the past decade or so Portuguese sociologists are confronted with two slightly different institutional systems of incentives, both of which are nominally oriented towards 'internationalization'. At the national level, internationalization is understood to mean cross-national or transnational comparative research projects from a narrow disciplinary viewpoint. At the European level, however, funding is awarded to projects that go beyond the confines of any given discipline. Despite this important difference, institutional research funding agencies nowadays all privilege comparative, cross-national, and often post-disciplinary models of sociological research. Private foundations are no exception to this general trend. On several occasions since 2009, the Calouste Gulbenkian Foundation ran a Programme for the Internationalization of the Social Sciences.

DOI: 10.1057/9781137495518.0006

Discontinued owing to financial constraints, this programme was aimed at fostering the internationalization of the social sciences in Portugal, providing incentives for publication in international peer-reviewed journals. Partly as a result of these institutional incentives, and partly because it includes not only university staff but also high school teachers and sociologists who work for private companies and municipalities, the Portuguese professional association has grown from just 187 members in 1987 to 2,760 in 2012, being nowadays considered a 'very large' association by European standards (Neto 2013: 51; Fleck and Hönig 2015: 42; Agodi et. al. 2015), with a good degree of international exposure. A case in point was the organization of the 9th European Sociological Association's (ESA) Annual Meeting in Lisbon in 2009.

Finally, internationalization is also about *what* one studies. In my view, this is perhaps the most interesting aspect of the current phase of development of sociology in Portugal. As Portuguese sociologists have embraced this challenge, they have gradually been confronted with an expanded, more ambivalent conception of 'Portugal' itself, and its relative place in the community of nations. In short, internationalization has brought with it a transformation of the very sociological understanding of 'Portugal.' The principal reason for this has to do with the socially constructed nature of social reality. As materialist and positivist approaches in the 1970s and 1980s had constructed a sociologically coherent view of a class-based social formation with growing urban centres and a few industrial poles, post-positivist, critical, and culturalist approaches that have gained traction since the 1990s have been constructing a very different sociological portrait of Portugal. These approaches have had to confront the cultural trauma, and the silence around, the country's colonial past. The past, colonial or not, exists only if actively and carefully constructed in some present. To know the past involves breaking the silence which past events naturally inhabit. Yet to break the silence it is necessary for agents to make an active effort to remember. Historians, of course, play a major role in this. But so do other social scientists, not to mention citizens and politicians. Unfortunately, the glaring absence of race and ethnicity in Portuguese sociologists' chief teaching options and research topics speaks volumes about the enormous task that still lies ahead in this respect. As I write this, it is entirely possible for someone to graduate in sociology from a Portuguese university without having any contact whatsoever with the writings of W.E.B. Du Bois or Franz Fanon. This in a country which, despite its active role in the slave trade, has no

DOI: 10.1057/9781137495518.0006

museum dedicated to slavery and where media coverage of the topic is often cursory and self-congratulatory.

There are, however, a few encouraging signs. Portuguese critical and culturalist sociological approaches are at the forefront of the effort to remember and, in the process, to construct a more complicated and more realistic collective identity. As a result, a different 'Portugal' has been emerging in sociological circles that breaks with the collective silence around the colonial experience and which, by posing troubling questions about itself, generates invaluable social knowledge. Especially in the case of the post-positivist sociological analyses of the Coimbra school, this expanded understanding tends to incorporate a critical account of Portugal's post-colonial status (e.g. Santos 2004: 41 ff.). Hence Portugal has joined a series of former colonial powers that have had to deal with traumatic collective memories, which include slavery, colonialism, war, economic exploitation, and institutionalized racism. Current migratory flows of people, ideas, and objects only reinforce the need to develop an adequate sociological understanding of such post-colonial realities. Yet there is a fine line separating sociological approaches aimed at criticizing unjust social arrangements and outright activism. In my view, crossing that line entails compromising our explanations and curtailing attempts to deepen our understanding of the phenomena at hand (but see e.g. Burawoy 2005). I am of the view that one valid alternative involves analysing such phenomena from the perspective of a 'plural modernity' paradigm. More concretely, this involves studying phenomena such as racial discrimination within each specific variant of modernity and its entanglements with other variants over the course of history. In the case of Portugal, such a conceptual framework could be designated, lacking a better name, the 'Lusophone variant' of modernity. My assumption is that the historical trajectory of this Lusophone variant of modernity intersects with other variants but is distinctive enough, in terms of its cultural products, discursive formations, and so on, to merit independent analytical status. 'Portugal' thus becomes, in this light, a much larger, but also much more problematic, category than materialist, positivist models allow. It is a post-colonial, or post-imperial, society whose identity is Western European *and* African, Western European *and* South American, Western European *and* Asian, entanglements[10] that often incorporate conflict and, inevitably, the possibility of misunderstanding. I fear that without an adequate understanding of such entanglements, the sociology *of* Portugal will remain a radically incomplete project.

DOI: 10.1057/9781137495518.0006

Notes

1   Often in conjugation with Bourdieu's practice theory, again, an approach eminently amenable to empirical research.
2   http://theoryculturesociety.org/volker-h-schmidt-on-global-modernity/
3   See also the online platform on Portuguese social and political attitudes (IASPP): http://www.iaspp.ics.ul.pt/. See Barreto (2000) for a precursor in this attempt at compiling international socio-economic indicators.
4   The special issue 'The Mediterranean Welfare Regime and the Current Crisis' was published in volume 15, issue 4, 2013 (link: http://www.tandfonline.com/toc/reus20/15/4#.VbKcHnjjZVg).
5   There are currently 26 Associate Laboratories: see http://www.fct.pt/apoios/unidades/las.phtml.en#
6   http://alice.ces.uc.pt/en/
7   https://transrightseurope.com
8   http://www.ces.uc.pt/intimate/
9   https://www.fct.pt/apoios/index.phtml.en
10 On the notion of 'entanglement,' see Therborn (2003).

5
Sociology's Voices

Abstract: *In this chapter, Filipe Carreira da Silva presents excerpts from 16 interviews by leading Portuguese sociologists. 'Sociology's voices' is a collective discourse composed of first-hand accounts of the ways in which these sociologists have responded to three main problems: the initial attempts at the academic establishment of sociology in Portugal, as well as the experiences of political exile; the challenge of creating and establishing an academic discipline in a country emerging from political and social revolution; and how to respond to the challenges associated with the internationalization of science.*

Carreira da Silva, Filipe. *Sociology in Portugal: A Short History*. Basingstoke: Palgrave Macmillan, 2016. DOI: 10.1057/9781137495518.0007.

In this chapter I will pursue a slightly different model of exposition. Rather than imposing my authorial voice upon the object matter, I will give centre stage to the voices of sociologists who have been at the centre of the development of sociology in Portugal since 1945. I will, therefore, present relatively long excerpts from 16 interviews,[1] using second-voice commentary only to introduce the issues at stake. Besides selecting and editing these extracts, I am also responsible for having them translated into English. The interviews are organized into three main sections, each covering a different historical period: the early years; the period of institutionalization, and the current challenges facing sociology in Portugal.

The early years

Rui Pena Pires (1955) talks about the 'colonial question' by discussing his time in Angola in the early 1970s, specifically, how it was to grow up and study in a colonial society and his political engagement in anti-colonial movements.

> Question: Could you please talk about the experience of living in a colonial society, the war of independence, and your political involvement in that period?
>
> Answer: When I first arrived in Angola, I noticed that Portuguese colonial societies at the time had one particularity. Angola was not merely a non-democratic society for the colonized subject; it was a non-democratic society for everyone, including the colonizer. This means that the scope of permitted political participation was very, very narrow. As a result, when I first arrived at Luanda to study, all I wanted was to study and little else. Once in Luanda, I was fortunate enough to meet a number of classmates who were at the time trying to organize a students' union at the University of Luanda. Notice that, in Luanda, the government had forbidden the establishment of student unions in universities. There were student unions in Portugal, there were student unions in Mozambique, but there were not in Angola, because of what had happened in the other places. The solution for those who wanted to participate in student politics was to make up organizations that, taken together, equated with a student union. As a result, even though we did not have a student union as such, we had a cultural centre, a movie club, pedagogical missions as well as a coordinating committee that amounted, in practice, to the student union properly speaking. The older students with whom I joined in the creation of these voluntary organizations were ideologically Maoist, and this was how I entered politics in Angola. The university was a mostly

DOI: 10.1057/9781137495518.0007

white university. There were almost no black students in the university. For this reason, the most debated topics were those of student movements in Lisbon, Paris, or in any other place than properly those related to the colonial question or independence. There was also another particular feature of the political situation at the time in Angola. The PIDE,[2] the political police of the former regime, was quite tolerant towards the children of the colonizers, the young white population.... There was a kind of unwritten agreement. As long as the colonial question was not discussed, it was actually far easier for a university student in Luanda to talk about politics, even in Marxist terms, than in Lisbon. But that was the line, a line we eventually crossed in 1973. It was impossible not to talk about the colonial question once you have political debate. We eventually decided to tackle the colonial question by holding a debate on underdevelopment in Angola and publishing, in samizdat format, a collection of texts of mostly Latin-American authors, including Celso Furtado and Fernando Henrique Cardoso, André Frank, who had a book called *Latin America*, and Samir Amin who had worked on Africa. We went ahead with that publication. It was our first incursion into the colonial question. It was also our last, because afterwards all our activities were forbidden. (smile). This was because, somehow, even indirectly, we had crossed the line. (Pires 2014: 3)

Marinús Pires de Lima (1942) revisits his time as a student in Paris during the student revolts of May 1968. He also addresses his intellectual influences and contrasts the situation in Paris with that in Lisbon in the early 1970s.

Question: We may begin with your academic career. What would you highlight and how did you come across sociology?

Answer: My training in Paris proved decisive. I went there with two scholarships, one from the OECD and another from the Calouste Gulbenkian Foundation, both with the support of Adérito Sedas Nunes, who was my actual supervisor. He also gave me other crucial help, a letter of recommendation to Alain Touraine, who ended up supervising me in Paris. This was during May 1968, but the University of Paris never ceased to be a top university. Besides Touraine, I was taught by figures such as Michel Crozier, Georges Friedmann, Pierre Navile, Jean-Daniel Reynaud.... I went almost every year to Paris to talk to Touraine and to follow the seminars at the *École des hautes études en sciences sociales* at Nanterre. Nanterre, as you know, was at the heart of the May 1968 'événements', a development which marked my generation. Besides the cultural liberation, May 68 had fundamental political importance. It allowed us to compare, for the first time, the American empire, typified by the Vietnam War, and the Russian Empire, a socialist regime that

DOI: 10.1057/9781137495518.0007

was actually a dictatorship. I participated actively in these student revolts with Daniel Cohn-Bendit, who was a PhD student colleague of mine. This was how I got in touch with worlds hitherto unknown to me in Lisbon.

Question: How different was it from the situation in Portugal?

Answer: Completely different. In Portugal the ruler was Salazar, who would not even hear of talking about sociology. By April 25, 1974, I was a lecturer on a course called 'Social Aspects of Development' at ISCTE. It was in actual fact a course in sociology of development, but such a designation was forbidden. However, I benefited from the liberalization of the political regime under Marcelo Caetano. ... However, the cultural and political oppression that we were subjected to was still extremely violent. (Lima 2012: 937–38)

António Barreto (1942) talks about Sedas Nunes' ties to the Church and the public administration and the Sedas Nunes' cluster from the perspective of someone exiled in Switzerland but keen to remain informed of what was going on in Portugal.

Question: Let us begin with the people. Was there a Sedas Nunes' generation? What was it about?

Answer: I do not think there was a Sedas Nunes generation. There was Sedas Nunes, himself. And he made a generation. There were a dozen or two dozen social scientists supervised, or partially supervised, or chosen by him. In the 1960s I did not know him personally but his name and his work came to me in Geneva through *Análise Social* and the odd book. His trajectory is interesting and deserves a biography so as to understand how he achieved what he did. Tenacity was a central personal characteristic of his. He also knew very well the Portuguese public administration and, within it, the university and educational agencies responsible for research and development. And he had the support of a part of the Church. My guess is that towards the end of his life he was not so much related to the Church. But he still maintained close, individual, and personal relationships with very important figures within the ecclesiastical structure.

Question: How important was that?

Answer: It was crucial because it allowed him to navigate unconstrained within the world of public administration. If he would show up in the world of the social sciences, or in academia as a contrarian, a radical, or simply as a secular republican, they would not have let him proceed. The former regime reacted promptly and firmly against any attempt at observation and analysis of Portuguese society. We know of many people who tried to undertake sociological research but either vanished from the public eye or went on to study law or economics. Sedas Nunes benefited from that support, that blessing, so to speak. He associated himself gradually with the progressive Catholics. At

DOI: 10.1057/9781137495518.0007

that time, of course, it was the Communist Party that determined who was a progressive Catholic or not. At the time, the latter were *compagnons de route* of the Communists and Adérito Sedas Nunes was not with them. He was with JUC.[3] In JUC there was a group that included him, João Salgueiro, Bénard da Costa, Carlos Portas, Nuno Portas, Eduarda Cruzeiro, among others. This was a very important group of people who, despite not being properly 'progressive', were Catholic, democrats or liberals, who would emerge later on as the liberal wing of Marcelo Caetano. Slowly but steadily, Sedas Nunes managed to impose himself on this group.

I recall being in Switzerland and receiving in Geneva all the first volumes of *Análise Social* in one package, sent by my father. It included the famous number 7, the special double issue called 'Portugal, Developing Society'. It was a major contribution to the modernization of social thought about Portuguese society, industry, development problems, and Europe. That issue, absolutely fantastic, sold out almost immediately. It is a 500-page volume. You need to realize that, at the time, it was Adérito who determined the content of *Análise Social*. It was he who ordered articles from specific individuals, people he chose to write about a certain topic. ...

Adérito had the great merit of knowing how not to be stopped, of having religious, administrative, and political support. Moreover, because he was simultaneously interested in teaching at ISCTE and ISEG, he was able to send people abroad to do their PhDs. His explicit aim was that of creating a cluster of social scientists. He realized that, unless they graduated, they would not have been able to work on their own and gain experience. He proved himself able to think in the long-term. He knew how to wait and prepare himself, something rare in Portugal. (Barreto 2011: 416–17)

João Ferreira da Almeida (1941) addresses the period of institutionalization of sociology in Portugal, with a particular emphasis upon the historical discontinuity provided by the democratic transition of 25 April 1974.

Question: Would you please assess the development and consolidation of social science institutions in the last twenty, thirty years?

Answer: Well, I may make a brief incursion into a slightly more remote past regarding the origins of institutions such as GIS ...

Question: Exactly.

Answer: ... In fact, GIS basically represents the birth, or if you wish, the rebirth of sociology in the country. There were some essays in the period of the First Republic (1910–26), but these were on the whole incipient. It is, in fact, the birth of sociology in Portugal. And it is important to be born well, I believe.

DOI: 10.1057/9781137495518.0007

One of the elements that contributed to this healthy birth was the existence of some hybridism, that is, the small cluster around Sedas Nunes had very different academic backgrounds and different sorts of training. I believe that would characterize the first stages of development of our sociology, in this case positively. There were people trained in law, economics, literature, and so on. As a result, these births or rebirths, before April 1974, were made out of different disciplinary orientations. In the other social sciences, with different historical backgrounds, what happened was very different. History and ethnography, for instance, had old and rich traditions. In the case of anthropology, there was the old Institute nowadays known as ISCSP, whose concerns and empirical focus was on the colonies, even though there was also general training in anthropology as well. Anthropology has a very rich history, a history that dates back to the 1930s. Likewise, economics, demography, and linguistics all had established trajectories. By contrast, other domains in the social sciences, such as sociology, had to wait for April. But one can say that in all cases only after 1974 could you freely undertake research and publish your findings. ... Returning to the issue of the birth, I would say sociology had an auspicious beginning through GIS, since it was through it that the basic early training was made. It is always necessary to mention Sedas Nunes, who founded and promoted this process, directing, supporting, and encouraging this new generation, both in terms of research and teaching. Everything was being done in an almost artisanal, even risky fashion ... This is because there was no professional career, or, for that reason, any job security as such. We were all living off scholarships. We were people who had chosen to do that out of vocation, because that was what we really liked doing. (Almeida 2011: 502–03)

Hermínio Martins (1934) discusses the (unfulfilled) utopian energies unleashed by the social and political revolution of April 1974 by reference to the case of the then-nascent social sciences.

Question: For a long time, you were an exiled intellectual but you never ceased to follow attentively the thinking and political life in the country. What do you think about the consolidation of the social sciences in Portugal?

Answer: ... As to the consolidation of the social sciences in Portugal in the last thirty years, it is an established fact, moreover demonstrated by a vast array of occupational and bibliometric indicators. That was expected with the emerging of democracy, European integration, a certain material prosperity, and the growth in university student enrolment, not to mention the public incentives that since 1987 have been so important to stimulate scientific research in Portugal.

However, I must confess that I once had a utopian vision about this issue that I allowed myself to indulge with for some time after April 25, 1974. It was about the possibility of overcoming in Portugal some of the limitations in the

DOI: 10.1057/9781137495518.0007

division of scientific labour in cultural and social studies that I knew first-hand in the United Kingdom and North America. I refer to the hyper-specialiszation, i.e. the non-communication between disciplines or even between sub-disciplines, as well as the linguistic, cultural, and historical parochialism that characterized the intellectual universe of the social sciences. ... My utopian hope failed. The flaws that characterized the division of intellectual labour in Anglophone social sciences were reproduced not only mimetically, but with true and exacerbated zeal. How zealous the Portuguese academics proved to be in respect to the policing of cognitive, disciplinary, doctrinal, ideological, institutional, and corporative frontiers! Fortunately we can still rely upon multidisciplinary, polyglot, and cultured academics, including historically cultured ones, even though many of them have already retired or are about to. Has this generation worthy successors, with the same will to take on and relate various disciplinary perspectives? (Martins 2011: 463–64)

Institutionalization

José Madureira Pinto (1946) discusses one of the earliest sociological empirical studies in post-1974 Portugal, that is, the collaborative project with João Ferreira de Almeida on the issue of rural lease in Fonte Arcada, a rural community in Northwest Portugal.

> Question: Would you please describe your doctoral research, one of the first in the country. This is because this was a collaborative project with another sociologist, João Ferreira de Almeida, which began, I believe, during your time in GIS.
>
> Answer: ... The truth is that the circumstances (financial but also affective) surrounding the invitation, which João Ferreira de Almeida transmitted to me, for us to undertake a research project on rural sociology, made me promptly accept it. And there I go, making virtue and pleasure out of need, and with the support of my supervisor Boaventura de Sousa Santos, looking out for the right clues to sociologically penetrate the rural economy and society, with the more specific goal of understanding the persistence of rural leasing within the context of the changing social relations in Portugal's countryside. ... Since the available statistics at the time indicated the borough of Penafiel as one with the highest rates of rural leasing, we opted to choose one of its districts as our case study. The choice fell upon Fonte Arcada.
>
> In order to undertake this study, we resorted to techniques of gathering and treating information that would somehow recover the ethno-historiographical tradition of rural ethnography, adapting it to the properly sociological

DOI: 10.1057/9781137495518.0007

aims of analysis of processes of social reproduction/transformation following the revolutionary rupture of 1974. A survey applied to all domestic groups in the district, along with interviews and extended periods of direct observation of routinized interaction, work processes, daily mobility circuits, festive and religious rituals, allowing us to test our theoretical hypotheses. João Ferreira de Almeida focused mainly on the dynamics of reconfiguration of the class structure. ... I focused mainly on the symbolic-cultural and ideological dimensions of these same social processes, namely those which seemed to be especially relevant regarding social change: work, school, religiosity, and electoral politics. The study concluded with an analysis of the main cycle of local festivities ... about the effect of the on-going class changes in that community on the meaning-making forms involved in socially differentiated ways of dealing with the main moments of the festivity cycle. (Pinto 2013: 693–94)

João Freire (1942) discusses his first years in the sociology department at ISCTE, namely the challenge of obtaining academic credentials and his own PhD on the historical sociology of anarcho-syndicalism in Portugal.

Question: Let us come back to your academic trajectory, even before your doctorate.

Answer: Very well. In 1977 and 1978, the problem of obtaining PhDs emerges. We did not have anyone with a PhD in the department. The one closest to obtaining one was Teresa Sousa Fernandes, with a PhD from Brandeis in the United States, but she was still to complete it. As a result, I showed interest in pursuing one. What I should have studied was the co-operative movement, since in Portugal at the time agrarian reform was in full swing and we had numerous self-managed companies. That was also what I was teaching at the time – sociology of work, co-operativism. This was really what I wanted to do. But there were no resources. There was no money to undertake a survey. All you had was a sabbatical leave, but no financial support to do research. It is around this time that the CIES ('Centro de Investigação e Estudos de Sociologia') was created. The aim was to have it accredited by the National Institute of Scientific Research (INIC) as it was then, but this eventually failed. Hence my dilemma: How am I to work without the necessary instruments? I could not afford to hire anyone, research assistants, nothing. This is when I thought of an alternative, despite being aware of the risk of being interpreted as asking a favour of my political friends, to make use of my contacts among the old militants of the libertarian syndicalist movement, the old anarcho-syndicalism, in order to study, from a historical-sociological perspective, work, namely industrial work, syndicalism and the ideologies of the time. And that was what I did. (Freire 2010: 27–28)

DOI: 10.1057/9781137495518.0007

Maria de Lourdes Rodrigues (1956) talks about her experience of being in the first cohort of sociology students at ISCTE in the aftermath of 25 April 1974.

Question: On April 25 1974 you are 18 years old, right?

Answer: Yes.

Question: What do you recall from that period? How did it affect you?

Answer: What I recall is that all doors that used to be closed were, all of a sudden, wide open. Suddenly, the world is a different place and it is possible to live, travel, to do things... everything is transformed. I recall that overwhelming sensation vividly. Also, I remember to go on a high school finalists' trip, organized in completely new terms. Everything was done with excitement, but the most important memory I have of those days is that of freedom. Suddenly, everyday life changed, but also our very expectations. Nineteenth-seventy-four is the year I went to college, here at ISCTE, which had been created the year before as a management school, a social sciences and management institute. There were no courses in sociology, for reasons well known. And I recall before applying to the university talking with my friends about a dazzling new degree in sociology that was about to open. And it is in ISCTE, whose precarious installations were down in Entrecampos in a little building where I begin my academic career. And I pursued it until 1977. These first three years had the particularity of being a common stream to the degrees in management and economics. As a result, classes were quite large, with students reading management and economics. Only after the third year did you specialize. As to my recollections, in that context of great instability and uncertainty, there were two lecturers who stood out. In certain courses, lectures were given by five or six different people whom we barely had the chance of knowing. But there were lecturers who had a more regular presence. One is Eduarda Cruzeiro, who taught social analysis. The other was Miriam Halpern Pereira, who taught history. For those in my generation, both become sort of references in terms of teaching quality and attention to the students' needs.... (Rodrigues 2015: 6–7)

Helena Carreiras (1965) talks about her experience as a sociology student in the early 1980s, discussing not only the theoretical references of the time (Bourdieu, Giddens) but also the role of the military in the country and as an object of sociological research.

Question: How was your undergraduate degree?

Answer: ... At the end of my degree, after having gone through the heritage of Bourdieu and Giddens, with their attempts at syntheses between structure and agency, between the material and the symbolic, approaches that may be difficult to apply empirically but provide an invaluable integrated view of

DOI: 10.1057/9781137495518.0007

society, partly because of my interest in issues of power and conflict, there were circumstances that would prove decisive in defining what came next. At the time, Maria Carrilho, who was to become my supervisor and with whom I worked in my first incursions into the universe of the military, was offering a seminar on the sociology of military institutions. And then it occurred to me: Well, I should do this course because if I am so interested in power and violence, there is nothing better than to study the setting and the agents of the institution responsible for managing collective violence. And so I did. I did that seminar and subsequently I did my degree dissertation on youth and military service in Portugal, where I explored the perspective of the relation between society and the armed forces. That was how I started working on that universe, a very interesting one as it turns out. I kept on studying the military since it is a privileged platform to study both local social dynamics and those taking place outside the military, especially because the military have gradually opened up to society. It works as a magnifying lens that amplifies many of the dynamics outside. In Portugal, moreover, it is a particularly interesting object of study because the military were the protagonists of a democratic revolution. By contrast, in most other countries, the military are not exactly the most attractive objects of study. (Carreiras 2011: 10)

Eduarda Cruzeiro (1937) talks about her PhD dissertation on student folklore under the supervision of Pierre Bourdieu, part and parcel of a larger intellectual collaboration that would span several decades.

Question: A dissertation supervised by Bourdieu... How did that happen?

Answer: It was through Sedas Nunes who, in a first phase, was the main disseminator of Pierre Bourdieu's theories in Portugal. Adérito had established many contacts in Paris, including with Bourdieu, Alain Touraine, Henri Mendras. In 1968–69 I went to Paris, contacted Bourdieu in order to attend his seminar and he accepted me. I interrupted my studies in 1969–70 to get married, but I returned in 1971–72 and started thinking about the topic of my dissertation. At this period, Bourdieu was very interested in studying university staff in France and suggested that I work on university teaching staff in Portugal. At the time, since there was no public research funding, he was of the view that one should study sociological issues that could potentially be of interest to the administrative apparatus. Bourdieu's advice to me was that I would contact the Ministry of Education with the suggestion of doing a survey, which would also be of administrative interest to the Ministry. I returned to Portugal and discussed this with Sedas Nunes, who then facilitated my way into the Ministry of Education. A survey and the respective funding followed, and a working group in the Ministry was eventually established. However, with the change of the Director-General of higher education who wanted to revise everything without consulting

DOI: 10.1057/9781137495518.0007

anyone, the project came to a halt. April 25 happened soon afterwards and the project was abandoned. Deciding not to go through the same experience of wasting a year-and-a-half of work, I changed my research topic to a more historical perspective – the history of the origins of the dual high school system in Portugal that goes back to the early nineteenth century. Bourdieu was not impressed by this new topic and, since he was then interested in symbolic agency in schools, suggested that I studied student traditions. I first thought of it as almost nonsense: How could you study student folklore sociologically, especially someone who was so sceptical of student initiation rituals? But soon afterwards I started working on the topic, got carried away with it, and this is what I eventually ended up doing. (Cruzeiro 2011: 450–51)

Current challenges

Boaventura de Sousa Santos (1940) talks about Marxism in sociology, namely the latest crisis of Marxism that propels a critical engagement with Marx's Eurocentrism through a non-Western lens.

Question: How do you see the trajectory of Marxism and Marxist debates by reference to sociology? Do you think there is a waning of the influence of Marxism upon the social sciences?

Answer: Well, the presence of Marxism in sociology is nowadays an established fact in every department I know of, except for those either confessional or very conservative. Marx is one of the founders of the discipline and the inspiring figure of one of its currents. … Marxism's crises occur in different periods for different reasons. The first crisis was right after Lukács. … The second crisis of Marxism was when we reached the 1980s, with the debacle of the Soviet system, the crisis of Western Marxism, and the decline of social democracy. … The third crisis of Marxism, maybe the deepest yet, took place with the World Social Forum. The diversity of social movements fighting for a better world became evident. Many of them were not Marxist in any meaningful way, did not use its concepts, and were even hostile when they learnt them. This process had two major virtues. The first was to deepen the ecological critique of Marxism … Now it was these rural, nativist, and social movements who asked: What is that idea of the infinite development of productive forces? That means extractivism, destruction of our communities, destruction of our water, of our forests, of our biodiversity. And suddenly, Marx was a Eurocentric. … The other virtue was to divulge to a wider public high quality Marxist intellectuals who had been ignored because they did not speak, or wrote in French not in English, and who lived or still live in India

DOI: 10.1057/9781137495518.0007

or Latin America. Of those I know best José Maria Mariátegui and Álvaro Garcia Liñera. (Santos 2012: 707–08)

José Machado Pais (1953) talks about Simmel and Goffman as the main intellectual influences who have shaped his approach to the sociology of everyday life.

> Question: If you had to highlight a work, a book that had influenced you the most, what would that be?
>
> Answer: Simmel was an author who exerted a great influence over me: The Philosophy of Money, Feminine Culture. Simmel and Goffman: Interaction Rituals and The Representation of the Self in Everyday Life. They are the walking sticks that help me move forward to what would become my second book: *As Formas de Amar da Burguesia* ('The ways of Loving of the Bourgeoisie') was a journey with Goffman and Simmel. Simmel was the first sociologist to really study the seduction rituals, the coquette, the rituals of gallantry in *Feminine Culture*. What I effectively found out was something that Simmel had already point to, namely that seduction rituals are rituals that to subsist they need not to be oriented to the attainment of a goal.
>
> Question: Sociability is the end itself?
>
> Answer: Exactly. They are actions that we could designate as sociophiliac, not oriented towards pursuing a certain goal. No. It is philia, it is sociability, it is conviviality, it is to want to seduce for its own sake, not seducing as a means to attain an end. It was this ambivalence, about which Simmel writes about when he discusses the rituals of coquetry, that I came across in my study of the seduction rituals of the nineteenth century bourgeoisie. For instance, some minuets clearly show that ambivalence of negative and positive hypotheses that converge towards the 'maybe'. It is not by chance that Simmel is considered to be the sociologist of the 'maybe'. Let me see if I recall an example. 'Mister Naughty, do you want a kiss? You won't get one. But sit by my side.' So the coquette begins by portraying herself as innocent. 'Mister Naughty'. He is the naughty one, not her. But it is she who challenges him: 'Mister Naughty, do you want a kiss?'. She advances with the possibility of a kiss. But then what does she say? She retracts: 'Mister Naughty, do you want a kiss? You won't get one.' But then she moves forward again: 'But sit by my side'. It is, in short, a game of moving forward and backwards. As I said, it is about an ambivalence that is fed upon by negative and positive possibilities that converge upon the maybe. And it is this 'maybe' that feeds, after all, the ritual of seduction. (Pais 2011: 32–33)

Maria de Lourdes Lima dos Santos (1935) revisits the origins of the Observatory of Cultural Activities, whose creation in 1996 illustrated a more general trend towards policy-oriented social research.

DOI: 10.1057/9781137495518.0007

Question: How was that change from a more strictly academic profile to a more explicit concern with public policy?

Answer: Right. The emergence of the Observatory of Cultural Activities. ... In 1995 the first socialist government of António Guterres created a Ministry of Culture whose minister was a university professor, Manuel Maria Carrilho. ... When I eventually called him back to let him know that I was not accepting his invitation to create an observatory in the domain of the arts and culture, I changed my mind at the last minute. 'Will you accept my invitation?', he asked. 'Yes, I will', was my reply. (smile) What was the purpose of the observatory? To begin with, it was not part of the Ministry. It was, and remains, a non-profit association, with three founding institutional partners: the University of Lisbon, through the ICS where I was based; the INE, our national statistics institute, and the Ministry of Culture itself, which supported the functioning and provided the installations. ... I think the OAC was a contribution to the sociology of culture to start with, regarding job opportunities as well as the study of various aspects of cultural life in Portugal. That was actually the central aim of the observatory, to undertake research and divulge it. The OAC had, and still has, various publication outlets, including a research series that publishes the results of the main projects. (Santos 2010: 16–17)

Manuel Villaverde Cabral (1940) makes use of his own more recent research experience to talk about how money affects the production of sociological knowledge today.

Question: Let us return to your sociology...

Answer: Let us return to my own involvement. Until 2001, my work was not money-driven, but in the last ten years or so most of my work has been commissioned. ...

Question: Looking at the sociology that is being done today in Portugal, is there a risk of researchers losing their autonomy regarding the definition of their agenda?

Answer: Obviously, there is a risk... After all the work we had in distinguishing between a social problem and a sociological problem, we fell once again upon social problems, not only because they exist and are urgent but also because there is money to study them. This will be the future of a great part of the social sciences, of sociology, in particular of social psychology: to inquire into social problems simply because that is where the money is. Money for basic research in the social sciences, in sociology, in political science, I do not believe there will be much. By contrast, there will always be organizations willing to pay for studies of electoral outcomes, housing problems, and health care issues, such as ageing. (Cabral 2011: 533–35)

DOI: 10.1057/9781137495518.0007

Anália Torres (1954) comments upon her experience as President of the Portuguese National Association of Sociology (2002–07), including Michael Burawoy's enthusiastic reaction to the 'public' character of sociology in Portugal.

> Question: Could you please describe the central aspects of your international experience?[4]
>
> Answer: My experience comes from working in research networks as well as from attending congresses and being actively engaged at the associational level. A case in point is the fact that I have been President of the Portuguese Association of Sociology, which put me in direct contact with other national association presidents and, at a more global level, with the International Sociological Association. (.. My mandate was from 2002 and 2007. At this time, sociology in Portugal is very different from what it used to be in the 1990s. There was already a certain public recognition of sociology at the national level. At one point, I was invited to go to the US, partly because at the time I was also a member of the Board of European Sociological Associations. I met Michael Burawoy, and invited him to visit Portugal. ... Michael Burawoy came in 2006, around the time I had organized a national event on sociology as a science and as an occupation. He was very impressed with what he saw. He said: 'You are the poster child of public sociology!' This is because he saw sociologists in political office, and he asked me: 'How did you manage to do this?' I said: 'It was them who approached me with a request; we then conducted a survey and provided the results in six months, and that was it.' He seemed puzzled with all this commissioned research. And then he said something I have been using a lot, that we were the most vibrant sociology in Europe. (Torres 2013: 30–31).

Notes

1   These interviews originate from two sources. One is the journal *Análise Social* and the other is the Brazilian-Portuguese-Mozambican project 'Cientistas Sociais de Língua Portuguesa: Histórias de Vida' (http://cpdoc.fgv.br/cientistassociais/lista). I would like to thank Ricardo Carvalho for having told me about this project. The reference for each interview is provided in the bibliography. The title of this chapter takes its inspiration from Robert Fishman's book *Democracy's Voices*.

2   PIDE stands for: ' Polícia Internacional e de Defesa do Estado', or International and State Defence Police. It operated under this designation between 1945 and 1969. From 1969 until 1974 it changed its designation to DGS ('Direcção Geral de Segurança', or General Security Directorate), although it retained its

DOI: 10.1057/9781137495518.0007

competences and modus operandi. The dismantlement of PIDE-DGS was one of the first priorities of the new political regime in 1974.

3   JUC is the acronym for 'Juventude Universitária Católica' ('Catholic University Youth').

4   My own formulation.

DOI: 10.1057/9781137495518.0007

Conclusion: Sociology in Portugal in the Twenty-First Century

Abstract: *Filipe Carreira da Silva concludes with some brief remarks about the challenges facing sociology in Portugal in the near future. His argument develops in three successive steps. First, recent data on enrolments and graduations in sociology is presented. Second, he discusses how these figures reflect the impact of austerity policies following the 2011 external intervention by the Troika and the ensuing economic crisis. Third, he considers the extent to which breaking the disciplinary silences considered above might contribute to a successful overcoming of these difficulties.*

Carreira da Silva, Filipe. *Sociology in Portugal: A Short History*. Basingstoke: Palgrave Macmillan, 2016.
DOI: 10.1057/9781137495518.0008.

DOI: 10.1057/9781137495518.0008

Seven years on, most Europeans still grapple with the effects of the financial crisis of 2008: budget deficits and public debt; shrinking economies; insufficient job creation; high unemployment; increased labour market vulnerability; and rising inequality. Despite being widespread, these effects are stronger in some countries than in others. Bailed-out Portugal has been one of Europe's hardest hit nations. The implementation of the austerity package brokered between the Portuguese government and the so-called Troika – the three international organizations (the IMF, the European Commission, and the European Central Bank) from which the country sought financial assistance – in the spring of 2011 implied various cutbacks and significant changes to social benefits. These occurred as the Portuguese economy faced its worst downturn since the mid-1970s, with unemployment and the risk of being atypically employed reaching record levels, and demand for social welfare provision expanding at an equal pace. Unemployment in Portugal ranked amongst the highest in the EU, with the average unemployment rate jumping from 7.6% in 2008 to the record high of 17.8% in April 2013, with youth unemployment peaking at 42.5%.[1] In addition, the combination of high insider employment protection with high labour market dualization, that is, an increasing separation between insiders and outsiders (Beramendi et al. 2015: 108), has created an ideal scenario for mass emigration and job precariousness among young sociology graduates in Portugal. Although figures for emigration of sociologists are difficult to obtain, there is reliable data concerning enrolments in sociology degrees and their unemployment rates.

Let me briefly discuss the main five sociology undergraduate degrees from this perspective. The oldest and most reputed sociology degree, the one at ISCTE, seems to maintain its lead, attracting a relatively large number of students (70) while guaranteeing the smallest unemployment rate: 6.3% against a 11.3% national average among other social sciences graduates. In 2013–14, 67% of students studying sociology in ISCTE were women, and the entry requirement was among the highest in the country (percentile: 63%). Also in Lisbon, the sociology degree offered in the New University accepts fewer students (55), with a lower entry requirement (percentile: 55%), but ensures a similarly good level of employability to its graduate students (unemployment: 6.6%). Outside the capital, the situation is arguably worse. In particular, the unemployment figures are noticeably higher. In Coimbra, a smaller cohort of students (41, 57% of which are women), with a satisfactory entry requirement (percentile: 61%), faces the worst employability scenario: 21.7% of students were officially reported

DOI: 10.1057/9781137495518.0008

as unemployed in December 2014. In Évora and Algarve, in the Southern part of the country, the situation is not much different. With unemployment figures of 21.6% and 16.4%, students graduating in sociology from these universities are facing a hard time getting a job. In the North of the country, in Oporto, the situation is equally difficult. Even though the entry requirement for sociology in the University of Porto is the highest in the country (percentile: 70%), its unemployment rate (16.5%) is over twice as much as in the two Lisbon universities considered here.[2]

These figures suffice to illustrate the impact of the economic crisis on the profession. Although a sociology degree provides some protection against unemployment, the fact remains that in some cases young Portuguese sociologists can be facing unemployment rates of over 20%. Doctoral and post-doctoral scholarships have provided a partial solution to this problem. Between 1994 and 2012, the Portuguese Foundation for Science and Technology awarded 4.352 doctoral scholarships to students in the social sciences, including sociology. Since 2010, however, these figures have been diminishing.[3] Unsurprisingly, an increasing number of Portuguese sociologists were left with no option but to pursue an academic career abroad.

For those who remained in Portugal, there is at least one challenge. This challenge consists of pursuing the development of sociology in Portugal while avoiding the blind spots and disciplinary silences that marked earlier stages of its process of development. This is, no doubt, a daunting challenge, especially given the demanding financial constraints facing higher education institutions in the country. But it is, nonetheless, a necessary one. If Portuguese sociologists want to keep having their voices heard in the multiple international outlets they have been participating in in the last few decades, sociology of Portugal needs to be truly able to address the epistemological, theoretical, and methodological challenges of plural modernity.

Notes

1   Eurostat figures.
2   Data available in here: http://infocursos.mec.pt.
3   https://www.fct.pt/apoios/bolsas/estatisticas/dados/TbB82.xls

DOI: 10.1057/9781137495518.0008

References

Abbott, A. (1999) *Department and Discipline: Chicago Sociology at One Hundred*. Chicago: The University of Chicago Press.

Abbott, A. (2001) *The Chaos of Disciplines*. Chicago: The University of Chicago Press.

Abbott, A. and J. Sparrow (2007) 'Hot War, Cold War: The Structures of Sociological Action, 1940–1955', in: C. Calhoun (ed.) *Sociology in America: A History*. Chicago: Chicago University Press.

Adcock, R., M. Bevir and S. Stimson (eds.) (2007) *Modern Political Science: Anglo-American Exchanges since 1880*. Princeton: Princeton University Press.

Ágoas, F. (2013) 'Narrativas em perspetiva sobre a história da sociologia em Portugal', *Análise Social* 206, 221–56.

Agodi, M.C. et al. (2015) 'Report on National Sociological Associations in Europe', *European Societies* 17, 3, 281–300.

Alexander, J.C. (1987) *Twenty Lectures. Sociological Theory since World War II*. New York: Columbia University Press.

Alexander, J.C. et al. (eds.) (2004) *Cultural Trauma and Collective Identity*. Berkeley: University of California Press.

Almeida, J.F. (1976) *A Investigação nas Ciências Sociais*. Lisboa: Presença.

Almeida, J.F. (1986) *Classes sociais nos campos: camponeses parciais na região do Noroeste*. Lisboa: Instituto de Ciências Sociais.

Almeida, J.F. (1988) 'Discurso de Abertura', *Análise Social* 100, 467–74.

Almeida, J.F. (1991) 'Ciências Sociais', in: J.M. Gago (ed.) *Ciência em Portugal*. Lisboa: Imprensa Nacional – Casa da Moeda.

Almeida, J.F. and J.M. Pinto (1976) *A Investigação nas Ciências Sociais*. Lisboa: Ed. Presença.

Almeida, J.F. and J.M. Pinto (1986) 'Da Teoria à Investigação Empírica. Problemas Metodológicos Gerais', in: Silva, A.S. and J.M. Pinto (eds.) *Metodologia das Ciências Sociais*. Porto: Afrontamento, 55–78.

Almeida, J.F. and A.F. Costa (1990) *Valores e Representações Sociais*. Lisboa: Fundação Calouste Gulbenkian.

Almeida, J.F. (2011) 'Entrevista a João Ferreira de Almeida por Renato Miguel do Carmo', *Análise Social* 200, 500–21.

Antoine, J. (2005) *Histoire des sondages*. Paris: Editions Odile Jacob.

Ash, M. and A. Söllner (eds.) (1996) *Forced Migration and Scientific Change: Émigré German-Speaking Scientists and Scholars After 1933*. Cambridge: Cambridge University Press.

Bannister, R. (2005) 'Sociology', in: T. Porter and D. Ross (eds.) *The Cambridge History of Science*. Cambridge: Cambridge University Press, 329–53.

Barreto, A. (ed.) (1996) *A Situação Social em Portugal, 1960–1995*. Lisboa: Instituto de Ciências Sociais da Universidade de Lisboa.

Barreto, A. (ed.) (2000) *A Situação Social em Portugal 1960–1999. Volume II. Indicadores Sociais em Portugal e na União Europeia*. Lisboa: Imprensa de Ciências Sociais.

Barreto, A. (2011) 'Entrevista a António Barreto por Marina Costa Lobo', *Análise Social* 200, 414–29.

Beck, U., A. Giddens and S. Lash (1994) *Reflexive Modernization. Politics, Tradition and Aesthetics in the Modern Social Order*. Cambridge: Polity Press.

Beck, U. (2000) *What is Globalization?* Cambridge: Polity.

Benoist, J-M. (1978) *The Structural Revolution*. London: Weidenfeld & Nicolson.

Beramendi, P. et al. (2015) 'Introduction: The Politics of Advanced Capitalism', in: P. Beramendi et al. (eds.) *The Politics of Advanced Capitalism*. Cambridge: Cambridge University Press, 1–65.

Bulmer, M. (1984) *The Chicago School of Sociology. Institutionalization, Diversity and the Rise of Sociological Research*. Chicago: Chicago University Press.

Burawoy, M. (2005) 'For Public Sociology', *American Sociological Review* 70, 4–28.

DOI: 10.1057/9781137495518.0009

Cabral, M.V. (2011) 'Entrevista a Manuel Villaverde Cabral por José Neves', *Análise Social* 200, 522–37.

Cabral, M.V., J. Vala and J. Freire (eds.) (2000) *Trabalho e Cidadania.* Lisboa: Imprensa de Ciências Sociais.

Cabral, M.V., F.C. Silva and T. Saraiva (2008) *Cidade e Cidadania. Governança urbana e participação cidadã em perspectivas comparadas.* Lisboa: Imprensa de Ciências Sociais.

Calhoun, C. (ed.) (2007) *Sociology in America.* Chicago: University of Chicago Press.

Cardoso, J.L. (2011) 'Vitorino Magalhães Godinho and the Annales School: History as a way of Thinking', *e-Journal of Portuguese History* 9, 2, 105–14.

Cardoso, J.L. (2013) 'O Gabinete de Estudos Corporativos (1949–1961) e a génese de uma biblioteca moderna de ciências sociais', *Análise Social* 206, 193–216.

Carreiras, H. (2011) 'Helena Carreiras (interview)'. Rio de Janeiro, CPDOC/FGV;LAU/IFCS/UFRJ; ISCTE/IUL, 2011. 40 p. Available at: http://cpdoc.fgv.br/sites/default/files/cientistas_sociais/ helena_carreiras/TranscricaoHelenaCarreiras.pdf

Casanova, J. (1996) 'Campo sociológico e publicação – a revista Sociologia, Problemas e Práticas (1986–1996)', *Sociologia, Problemas e Práticas* 20, 131–68.

Clark, T.N. (1972) 'The Stages of Scientific Institutionalization' *International Social Science Journal* 24, 658–71.

Clark, T.N. and P. Clark (1971) 'Le patron et son cercle: clef de l'Université française'. *Revue française de sociologie* 12, 1, 19–39.

Chernilo, D. (2006) 'Social Theory's Methodological Nationalism: Myth and Reality' *European Journal of Social Theory* 9, 1, 5–22.

Cohen-Cole, J. (2009) 'The Creative American: Cold War Salons, Social Science, and the Cure for Modern Society', *Isis* 100, 219–62.

Collini, S. (1988) 'Discipline History and Intellectual History: Reflections on the historiography of the social sciences in Britain and France', *Revue de Synthese* 101, 387–99.

Connell, R.W. (1997) 'Why is Classical Theory Classical?', *American Journal of Sociology* 1026, 1511–57.

Coser, L. (1971) *Masters of Sociological Thought. Ideas in Historical and Social Context.* New York: Harcourt Brace Jovanovich.

Coser, L. (1984) *Refugee Scholars in America: Their Impact and their Experiences.* New Haven: Yale University Press.

DOI: 10.1057/9781137495518.0009

Costa, A.F. (1988) 'Cultura Profissional dos Sociólogos', *Sociologia –
Problemas e Práticas* 8, 107–24.

Costa, A.F. and F.L. Machado (1998), 'Processos de uma modernidade
inacabada: mudanças estruturais e mobilidade social', in: J.M.L.
Viegas and A.F. Costa (eds.), *Portugal, que Modernidade?* Oeiras, Celta
Editora, 17–44.

Cruz, A.B. (1983) *Para a História da Sociologia Académica em Portugal.*
Coimbra: Faculdade de Direito da Universidade de Coimbra.

Cruzeiro, E. (2011) 'Entrevista a Eduarda Cruzeiro por Luísa Schmidt'.
Análise Social 200, 446–59.

Dahrendorf, R. (1995) *LSE: A History of the London School of Economics
and Political Science, 1895–1995.* Oxford: Oxford University Press.

Dias, I. (2006) 'A Sociologia na Faculdade de Letras da Universidade do
Porto', *Sociologia* 16, 9–13.

Eisenstadt, S.N. (1963) *The Political Systems of Empires.* New York: The
Free Press.

Eisenstadt, S.N. (1968) 'Sociology' in: E. Shils (ed.) *International
Encyclopaedia of the Social Sciences.* New York: Macmillan.

Eisenstadt, S.N. (ed.) (2002) *Multiple Modernities.* New Brunswick, NJ:
Transaction Publishers.

Eisenstadt, S.N. (ed.) (2003) *Comparative Civilizations and Multiple
Modernities, Part II.* Leiden: Brill.

Eisenstadt, S.N. (2007) 'Múltiplas Modernidades. Ensaios', in P.T.
Almeida (ed.) *Colecção Estudos Políticos.* Lisboa: Livros Horizonte.

Elias, N. (1994) *Reflections on a Life.* Cambridge: Polity.

Fernandes, A.T. (1996) 'O Conhecimento Científico-Social: Elementos
para a Análise do seu Processo em Portugal', *Sociologia – Problemas e
Práticas,* 20, 9–41.

Fernandes, T.S. (1993) 'Modernidade e Geometrias Sociais. A
Representação da Ordem na Obra de Émile Durkheim'. *Cadernos de
Ciências Sociais* 12, 107–48.

Fernandes, T.S. (2008) 'Chemical Metaphors in Sociological Discourse.
Durkheim through the Imagery of Rousseau', *Journal of Classical
Sociology* 8, 4, 447–66.

Ferreira, N.E. (2006) *A Sociologia em Portugal: Da Igreja à Universidade.*
Lisboa: Imprensa de Ciências Sociais.

Fisher, D. (1993) *Fundamental Development of the Social Sciences:
Rockefeller Philanthropy and the United States Social Science Research
Council.* Ann Arbor: University of Michigan Press.

DOI: 10.1057/9781137495518.0009

Fleck, C. (2011) *A Transatlantic History of the Social Sciences. Robber Barons, the Third Reich and the Invention of Empirical Social Research.* London: Bloomsbury.

Fleck, C. (2015) 'Methodology of the History of the Social and Behavioral Sciences', in: James D. Wright (ed.) *International Encyclopedia of the Social and Behavioral Sciences*, 2nd edition. Elsevier.

Fleck, C. and C. Dayé (2015) 'Methodology of the History of the Social and Behavioural Sciences', in: J.T. Wright (ed.) *International Encyclopedia of the Social & Behavioral Sciences, 2nd edition.* Elsevier.

Fleck, C. and B. Hönig (2015) 'European Sociology. Its Size, Shape, and Excellence', in: S. Koniordos and A.-A. Kyrtsis (eds.) *Routledge Handbook of European Sociology.* Abingdon: Routledge, 40–66.

Fortuna, C. (2008) 'A internacionalização da Sociologia', in: *Sociedades Contemporâneas.* Porto: Afrontamento, 83–94.

Foucault, M. (1970) *The Order of Things: An Archaeology of the Human Sciences.* New York: Pantheon Books. (originally: 1966)

Foucault, M. [1971] (1991) 'Nietzsche, Genealogy, History', in: P. Rabinow (ed.) *The Foucault Reader.* London: Penguin, 76–100.

Foucault, M. [1975] (1991) *Discipline and Punish. The Birth of the Prison,* London: Penguin.

Foucault, M. (1982) 'On the Genealogy of Ethics', in: H. Dreyfus and P. Rabinow (eds.) *Michel Foucault.* Chicago: Chicago University Press, 229–52.

Freire, J. (2010) 'João Freire (interview, 2010). Rio de Janeiro, CPDOC/ FGV; LAU/IFCS/UFRJ; ISCTE/IUL. p.48 Available at: http:// cpdoc.fgv.br/sites/default/files/cientistas_sociais/joao_freire/ TranscricaoJoaoFreire14.05.2010.pdf

Garcia, J.L. et al. (2015) 'Portuguese sociology. A non-cesurial perspective', in: S. Koniordos and A.-A. Kyrtsis (eds.) *Routledge Handbook of European Sociology.* Abingdon: Routledge, 357–375.

Geary, D. (2008) 'Every Social Scientist her own Historian', *Modern Intellectual History* 5, 399–410.

Gibbons, M. et al. (1994) *The New Production of Knowledge: The Dynamics of Science and Research in Contemporary Societies.* London: Sage.

Giddens, A. (1971) *Capitalism and Modern Social Theory: An Analysis of the Writings of Marx, Durkheim and Max Weber.* Cambridge: Cambridge University Press.

Giddens, A. (1976) *New Rules of Sociological Method.* London: Hutchinson.

DOI: 10.1057/9781137495518.0009

Gilroy, P. et al. (1982) *The Empire Strikes Back – Race and Racism in '70s Britain*. London: Hutchinson/Centre for Contemporary Cultural Studies.

Gilroy, P. (1993) *The Black Atlantic: Modernity and Double Consciousness*. London: Verso.

Giner, S. and M.P. Yruela (2015) 'Contemporary Sociology in Spain', in: S. Koniordos and A.-A. Kyrtsis (eds.) *Routledge Handbook of European Sociology*. Abingdon: Routledge, 376–89.

Godinho, V.M. (1943–1946) *Documentos sobre a Expansão Portuguesa*. Lisbon: Editorial Gleba. (reprint: Lisbon: INCM, 2011).

Godinho, V.M. (1944) *A Expansão Quatrocentista Portuguesa*. Lisboa: Empresa Contemporânea de Edições. (reprint: Lisbon: Dom Quixote, 2008).

Godinho, V.M. (1946) *A Crise da História e as suas Novas Directrizes*. Lisboa: Empresa Contemporânea de Edições.

Godinho, V.M. (1955) *Prix et Monnaies au Portugal, 1750–1850*. Paris: Armand Collin.

Godinho, V.M. (1963) *Os Descobrimentos e a Economia Mundial*. Lisboa: Arcádia, 2 vols. (New edition, revised and enlarged: Editorial Presença: 1991, 4 vols)

Godinho, V.M. (1967) *Ensaios e Estudos*. Lisboa: Sá da Costa. (reprint: Lisbon: Sá da Costa, 2009–2010, vols 3).

Godinho, V.M. (1990) *Mito, Mercadoria, Utopia e Prática de Navegar*. Lisboa: Difel.

Goldthorpe, J. H. and D. Lockwood (1963) 'Affluence and the British Class Structure' *Sociological. Review* 11, 2, 133–63.

Goldthorpe, J.H., et al. (1968–69) *The Affluent Worker in the Class Structure*. Cambridge, Cambridge University Press.

Graham, L. and H. Makler (1979) *Contemporary Portugal: The Revolution and Its Antecedents*. Austin: University of Texas Press.

Guibentif, P. (2010) *Foucault, Luhmann, Habermas, Bourdieu; Une Génération Repense Le Droit*. Paris: LGDJ.

Habermas, J. ([1981] 1984) *The Theory of Communicative Action*, 2 vols. Cambridge: Polity Press.

Habermas, J. ([1980] 1997) 'Modernity: An Unfinished Project', in: M.P. d'Entréves and S. Benhabib (eds.) *Habermas and the Unfinished Project of Modernity*. Cambridge: MIT Press, 38–55.

Hall, S. (1992) *Culture, Media, Language. Working Papers in Cultural Studies, 1972–79*. London: Routledge.

DOI: 10.1057/9781137495518.0009

Hall, P. and D. Soskice (2001) *Varieties of Capitalism: The Institutional Foundations of Comparative Advantage*. Oxford: Oxford University Press.

Heilbron, J. (2004) 'A Regime of Disciplines: Toward a Historical Sociology of Disciplinary Knowledge', in: C. Camic and H. Joas (eds.) *The Dialogical Turn: New Roles for Sociology in the Postdisciplinary Age*. Lanham, MD: Rowman & Littlefield, 23–42.

Heilbron, J. et al. (2008) 'Toward a Transnational History of the Social Sciences', *Journal of the History of the Behavioral Sciences* 44, 146–60.

Hespanha, P. (1996) 'Os Custos e os Benefícios da Institucionalização Tardia da Sociologia em Portugal', *Oficina do CES*, 78, 1–18. Available at: http:www.ces.uc.pt/publicacoes/oficina/ficheiros/78.pdf

Hobsbawm, E.J. (1994) *The Age of Extremes. A History of the World, 1914–1991*. New York: Vintage.

Hoggarth, R. (1957) *The Uses of Literacy: Aspects of Working Class Life*. London: Chatto and Windus.

Inglehart, R. (1977) *The Silent Revolution: Changing Values and Political Styles Among Western Publics*. Princeton: Princeton University Press.

Isaac, J. (2007) 'The Human Sciences in Cold War America', *Historical Journal* 50, 725–46.

Isaac, J. (2012) *Working Knowledge: Making the Human Sciences from Parsons to Kuhn*. Cambridge, MA: Harvard University Press.

Isin, E. (1999) 'Introduction: Cities and Citizenship in a Global Age.' *Citizenship Studies* 3, 2, 165–71.

Keen, M. and J. Mucha (eds.) (1994) *Eastern Europe in Transformation. The Impact on Sociology*. Westport: Greenwood Press.

Keen, M. and J. Mucha (eds.) (2006) *Autobiographies of Transformation: Lives in Central and Eastern Europe*. London: Routledge.

Klein, J. (1990) *Interdisciplinarity: History, Theory and Practice*. Detroit: Wayne State University Press.

Klein, J., et al. (eds.) (2004) *Transdisciplinarity: Joint Problem Solving among Science, Technology, and Society – An Effective Way for Managing Complexity*. Basel: Birkhäuser.

Kuhn, T. (1962) *The Structure of Scientific Revolutions*. Chicago: Chicago University Press.

Kurzweil, E. (1980) *The Age of Structuralism: Levi-Strauss to Foucault*. London: Tavistock.

Lakatos, I. (1970) 'Falsificationism and the Methodology of Scientific Research Programmes', in: I. Lakatos and A. Musgrave (eds.) *Criticism and the Growth of Knowledge. Proceedings of the International*

DOI: 10.1057/9781137495518.0009

Colloquium in the Philosophy of Science, 1965, vol. 4. Cambridge: Cambridge University Press, 91–195.

Latour, B. (2005) *Reassembling the Social: An Introduction to Actor-Network-Theory.* Oxford: Oxford University Press.

Levine, D.N. (1996) *Visions of the Sociological Tradition.* Chicago: Chicago University Press.

Levi-Strauss, C. (1993) *Structural Anthropology, Part 1.* London: Penguin. (originally: 1963).

Levi-Strauss, C. (1994) *Structural Anthropology, Part 2.* London: Penguin. (originally: 1973).

Lima, M.P. (2012) 'Marinús Pires de Lima, um sociólogo do mundo do trabalho. Entrevista a Marinús Pires de Lima por Luísa Veloso', *Análise Social* 205, 937–45.

Lyotard, J.-F. [1979] (1984) *The Postmodern Condition. A Report on Knowledge.* Manchester: Manchester University Press.

Lobo, C. (1996) 'Os congressos de sociologia em Portugal', *Sociologia, Problemas e Práticas* 20, 113–30.

Machado, F.F. (1962) 'Sociologia em Portugal', *Expansão* 62, 1–2, 12–14.

Machado, F.L. (2009) 'Meio Século de Investigação Sociológica em Portugal', *Sociologia* 19, 283–343.

Marcel, J.-C. (1998) 'Jean Stoetzel élève de Maurice Halbwachs: les origines françaises de la théorie des opinions', *L'Année Sociologique* 48, 2, 319–51.

Marcel, J.-C. (2002) 'Le premier sondage d'opinion', *Revue d'Histoire des Sciences Humaines* 6, 145–53.

Martins, H. (1969) 'Opposition in Portugal', *Government and Opposition* 4, 2, 260–63.

Martins, H. (1971) 'Portugal', in: Margaret Archer and Salvador Giner (ed.) *Contemporary Europe: Class, Status, and Power.* London: Weidenfeld and Nicolson, 60–89.

Martins, H. (1974) 'Time and theory in sociology', in: J. Rex (ed.) *Approaches to sociology: an introduction to major trends in British sociology.* London: Routledge and Kegan Paul, 246–94.

Martins, H. (2011) 'Entrevista a Hermínio Martins por Helena Mateus Jerónimo', *Análise Social* 200, 460–83.

Mirowski, P. (2002) *Machine Dreams: Economics Becomes a Cyborg Science.* Cambridge: Cambridge University Press.

Mudrovcic, M.E. (1997) *Mundo Nuevo. Cultura y Guerra Fría en la Década del 60.* Rosario: Beatriz Viterbo.

DOI: 10.1057/9781137495518.0009

Neto, H.V. (2013) 'Principais estádios evolutivos da sociologia em Portugal', *Sociologia* 26, 37–59.

Nisbet, R. (1970) *The Social Bond. An Introduction to the Study of Society.* New York: Knopf.

Novick, P. (1988) *That Noble Dream. The 'Objectivity Question' and the American Historical Profession.* Cambridge: Cambridge University Press.

Nowotny, H., P. Scott and M. Gibbons (2001) *Re-thinking Science: Knowledge in an Age of Uncertainty.* Cambridge: Polity Press.

Nunes, A.S. (1954) *Situação e Problemas do Corporativismo.* Lisboa: Gabinete de Estudos Corporativos.

Nunes, A.S. (1961) *Princípios de Doutrina Social.* Lisboa: Livraria Morais Editora.

Nunes, A.S. (1964) 'Portugal, sociedade dualista em evolução', *Análise Social* 7–8, 407–62.

Nunes, A. S. (1965) 'Uma aproximação à Sociologia.' *Análise Social* 9–10, 7–72.

Nunes, A.S. (1982) *Sobre o Problema do Conhecimento nas Ciências Sociais. Materiais de uma Experiência Pedagógica.* Lisboa: Imprensa de Ciências Sociais.

Nunes, A.S. (1988) 'Histórias, uma história e a História – sobre a origem das modernas ciências sociais em Portugal', *Análise Social* 100, 11–55.

Nunes, A.S. (2000) *Antologia Sociológica.* Lisboa: Imprensa de Ciências Sociais.

Nunes, A.S (2013) *O GIS e a Análise Social na Abertura da Sociedade Portuguesa.* Lisboa: Imprensa de Ciências Sociais.

Pais, J. M. (2011) *José Machado Pais (interview, 2010).* Rio de Janeiro, CPDOC/FGV; LAU/IFCS/UFRJ; ISCTE/IUL; IIAM. 28 pp. Available at: http://cpdoc.fgv.br/sites/default/files/cientistas_sociais/jose_machado_pais/TranscricaoJoseMachadoPais.pdf

Pais, J. M. and M. V. Cabral (2006) 'Sociología en Portugal', in: S. Giner, E. Lamo de Espinosa and C. Torres (eds.) *Diccionario de Sociología.* 2nd edition. Madrid: Alianza Editorial.

Picó, J. (2003) *Los Años Dorados de la Sociología (1945–1975).* Madrid: Alianza.

Pinto, J.M. (1984) 'Epistemologia e Didáctica da Sociologia', *Revista Crítica de Ciências Sociais* 14, 47–75.

Pinto, J.M. (1985) *Estruturas sociais e Práticas simbólico-ideológicas nos Campos. Elementos de Teoria e de Pesquisa Empírica.* Porto: Afrontamento.

DOI: 10.1057/9781137495518.0009

Pinto, J.M. (1994) *Propostas para o Ensino das Ciências Sociais*. Porto: Afrontamento.

Pinto, J.M. (2004) 'Formação, tendências recentes e perspectivas de desenvolvimento da sociologia em Portugal', *Sociologia - Problemas e Práticas* 46, 11–31.

Pinto, J.M. (2007) *Indagação Científica, Aprendizagens Escolares, Reflexividade Social*. Porto: Afrontamento.

Pinto, J.M. (2013) 'Da sociologia como profissão à sociologia crítica. Entrevista com José Madureira Pinto por Renato Miguel do Carmo e Virgílio Borges Pereira', *Análise Social* 208, 685–720.

Pinto, J.M. and J. Queirós (eds.) (2010) *Ir e Voltar. Sociologia de uma Colectividade Local do Noroeste Português (1977-2007), vol. I*. Porto: Afrontamento.

Pinto, J.M. and A.S. Silva (eds.) (1986) *Metodologia das Ciências Sociais*. Porto: Afrontamento.

Pinto, J.M. and V.B. Pereira (eds.) (2007) *Pierre Bourdieu. A Teoria da Prática e a Construção da Sociologia em Portugal*. Porto: Afrontamento.

Pinto, P.R. (2011) 'Os trilhos da ciência política portuguesa: uma conversa com David Goldey', *Análise Social* 200, 605–10.

Pires, R.P. et al. (1984) *Os Retornados. Um Estudo Sociográfico*. Lisboa: Instituto de Estudos para o Desenvolvimento.

Pires, R.P. (2014) 'Rui Pires (interview, 2014). Lisboa, Portugal. CPDOC/ FGV; LAU/IFCS/UFRJ; ISCTE/IUL; IIAM. 29 pp. Available at: http://cpdoc.fgv.br/sites/default/files/cientistas_sociais/rui_pena/ TranscricaoRuiPena.pdf

Platt, J. (1996) *A History of Sociological Research Methods in America 1920-1960*. Cambridge: Cambridge University Press.

Polanyi, M. (1958) *Personal Knowledge*. London: Routledge.

Reed, A. (1997) *W.E.B. Du Bois and American Political Thought. Fabianism and the Color Line*. Oxford: Oxford University Press.

Rocha, E. (1984) 'Crescimento Económico em Portugal nos anos 1960–73: Alteração Estrutural e Ajustamento da Oferta à Procura de Trabalho', *Análise Social* 84, 621–44.

Rodrigues, M. L. (2015) 'Maria de Lurdes Reis Rodrigues (interview, 2013)'. Rio de Janeiro; LAU/IFCS/UFRJ; ISCTE/ IUL; IIAM. pp.52 Available at: http://cpdoc.fgv.br/sites/ default/files/cientistas_sociais/maria_lurdes_rodrigues/ TranscricaoMariaDeLurdesRodrigues.pdf

DOI: 10.1057/9781137495518.0009

Rohde, J. (2013) *Armed with Expertise: The Militarization of American Social Research during the Cold War*. Ithaca: Cornell University Press.

Ross, D. (2015) 'Changing Countours of the Social Sciences Disciplines', in: T. Porter and D. Ross (eds.) *The Cambridge History of Science*. Cambridge: Cambridge University Press, 205–36.

Said, E. (1979) *Orientalism*. New York: Vintage Books.

Santos, B.S. (1977) 'The Law of the Oppressed: The Construction and Reproduction of Legality in Pasargada Law', *Law and Society Review* 12, 5–126.

Santos, B.S. (1985) 'Estado e sociedade na semiperiferia do sistema mundial: o caso português', *Análise Social* 87–89, 869–901.

Santos, B.S. (1987) *Um Discurso sobre as Ciências*. Porto: Afrontamento.

Santos, B.S. (1989) *Introdução a uma Ciência Pós-Moderna*. Porto: Afrontamento.

Santos, B.S. (ed.) (1993) *Portugal: Um Retrato Singular*. Porto: Afrontamento.

Santos, B.S. (1994) *Pela Mão de Alice: O Social e o Político na Pós-Modernidade*. Porto: Afrontamento.

Santos, B.S. (2000) *A Crítica da Razão Indolente: Contra o Desperdício da Experiência*. Porto: Afrontamento.

Santos, B.S. (2004) 'Do Pós-Moderno ao Pós-Colonial. E para além de um e outro.' Keynote Address, VIII Congresso Luso-Afro-Brasileiro de Ciências Sociais, Coimbra. Available at: http://www.ces.uc.pt/ misc/Do_pos-moderno_ao_pos-colonial.pdf

Santos, B.S. (2012) 'O Intelectual de Retaguarda. Entrevista com Boaventura de Sousa Santos por Helena Mateus Jerónimo e José Neves', *Análise Social* 204, 685–711.

Santos, M.L.L. (1988) 'Notícia', *Análise Social* 100, 463–66.

Santos, M.L.L. (2010) 'Maria de Lourdes Lima dos Santos. (interview, 2009)', Rio de Janeiro, CPDOC/FGV; LAU/IFCS/ UFRJ; ISCTE/IUL, 2010. 27 pp. Available at: http://cpdoc. fgv.br/sites/default/files/cientistas_sociais/maria_lourdes/ TranscricaoMariadeLourdesLimaSantos.pdf

Schmidt, V. (2006) 'Multiple Modernities or Varieties of Modernity?' *Current Sociology* 54, 1, 77–97.

Schmidt, V. (2007) 'One World, One modernity', in: V. Schmidt (ed.) *Modernity at the Beginning of the 21st Century*. Newcastle: Cambridge Scholars Press, 205–28.

DOI: 10.1057/9781137495518.0009

Schmidt, V. (2014) *Global Modernity. A Conceptual Sketch.* Basingstoke: Palgrave Macmillan.

Scott, J. (1990) *A Matter of Record. Documentary sources in social research.* Cambridge: Polity Press.

Shapin, S. and S. Schaffer (1985) *Leviathan and the Air-Pump: Hobbes, Boyle, and the Experimental Life.* Princeton: Princeton University Press.

Silva, A. (1996) 'A Sociologia em Évora', *Economia e Sociologia* 62, 111–20.

Silva, F.C. (2006) 'G.H. Mead in the History of Sociological Ideas', *Journal of the History of the Behavioral Sciences* 42, 1, 19–39.

Silva, F.C. (2007) 'Re-Examining Mead: G.H. Mead on the Material Reproduction of Society', *Journal of Classical Sociology* 7, 3, 291–313.

Silva, F.C. (2008) *Mead and Modernity: Science, Selfhood, and Democratic Politics.* Lanham, MD: Lexington Books.

Silva, F.C. (ed.) (2013) *Os Portugueses e o Estado-Providência. Uma Perspectiva Comparada.* Lisboa: Imprensa de Ciências Sociais.

Silva, A.S. and J.M. Pinto (eds.) (1986) *Metodologia das Ciências Sociais.* Porto: Afrontamento.

Silva, F.C. and M.B. Vieira (2009) 'Plural Modernity. Changing Modern Institutional Forms: Disciplines and Nation-states, *Social Analysis. The International Journal of Cultural and Social Practice* 53, 2, 60–79.

Skinner, Q. (1969) 'Meaning and Understanding in the History of Ideas', *History and Theory* 8, 1, 3–53.

Stocking, G. (1965) 'On the limits of presentism and historicism in the historiography of the behavioral sciences', *Journal of the History of the Behavioral Sciences* 1, 211–18.

Strathern, M. (2000) *Audit Cultures. Anthropological Studies in Accountability, Ethics, and the Academy.* London: Routledge.

Therborn, G. (2003) 'Entangled Modernities', *European Journal of Social Theory* 6, 3, 293–305.

Tomich, D. (2005) 'Vitorino Magalhães Godinho: Atlantic History, World History', *Review (Fernand Braudel Center)* 28, 4, In Honor of Vitorino Magalhães Godinho, 305–12.

Torres, A. (2013) 'Anália Torres (interview, 2013).' Lisboa, Portugal. CPDOC/FGV; LAU/IFCS/UFRJ; ISCTE/IUL; IIAM. pp.37 Available at: http://cpdoc.fgv.br/sites/default/files/cientistas_sociais/analia_torres/TranscricaoAnaliaTorres.pdf

Viegas, J.M. and A.F. Costa (eds.) (1998) *Portugal, Que Modernidade?* Lisboa: Celta.

DOI: 10.1057/9781137495518.0009

Vieira, M.B. and F.C. Silva (2013) 'Getting Rights Right. Explaining Social Rights Constitutionalization in Revolutionary Portugal.' *I*CON. International Journal of Constitutional Law* 11, 4, 898–922.

Wagner, P. (1990) *Sozialwissenchaften und Staat. Frankreich, Italien, Deutschland 1870–1980*. Frankfurt: Campus.

Wagner, P. (1994) *Sociology of Modernity. Liberty and Discipline*. London: Routledge.

Warwick, A. (2003) *Masters of Theory: Cambridge and the Rise of Mathematical Physics*. Chicago: Chicago University Press.

Wimmer, A. and N.G. Schiller (2002) 'Methodological nationalism and beyond: nation-state building, migration and the social sciences', *Global Networks* 2, 4, 301–34.

Yack, B. (1997) *The Fetishism of Modernities: Epochal Self-Consciousness in Contemporary Social and Political Thought*. Notre Dame: University of Notre Dame Press.

DOI: 10.1057/9781137495518.0009

Index

DOI: 10.1057/9781137495518.0010

DOI: 10.1057/9781137495518.0010

DOI: 10.1057/9781137495518.0010

DOI: 10.1057/9781137495518.0010

Lightning Source UK Ltd.
Milton Keynes UK
UKOW02n0350271115

263586UK00003B/14/P

9 781137 495501